**UNDERSTANDING
AND USING
ENGLISH
GRAMMAR**
Second Edition

CHARTBOOK

A Reference Grammar

Betty Schrampfer Azar

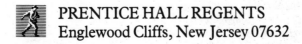
PRENTICE HALL REGENTS
Englewood Cliffs, New Jersey 07632

Library of Congress Cataloging-in-Publication Data

Azar, Betty Scrampfer, 1941-
    Understanding and using English grammar.   Chartbook : a reference
grammar / Betty Schrampfer Azar. -- 2nd ed.
        p.   cm.
    Includes index.
    ISBN 0-13-948233-4 (p)
    1. English language--Textbooks for foreign speakers.   2. English
Language--Grammar--1950-   I. Title.
PE1128.A973   1993
428.2'4--dc20
                                                        92-22548
                                                          CIP

Publisher: *Tina B. Carver*
Managing editor, production: *Sylvia Moore*
Editorial/production supervisor: *Janet Johnston*
Editorial assistants: *Shelley Hartle, Athena Foley*
Prepress buyer: *Ray Keating*
Manufacturing buyer: *Lori Bulwin*
Scheduler: *Leslie Coward*
Illustrator: *Don Martinetti*
Cover supervisor: *Marianne Frasco*
Cover designer: *Joel Mitnick Design*
Interior designer: *Ros Herion Freese*

© 1993 by PRENTICE HALL REGENTS
A Division of Simon & Schuster
Englewood Cliffs, New Jersey 07632

Printed in the United States of America

10 9 8 7 6 5 4 3 2 1

ISBN 0-13-948233-4

Prentice-Hall International (UK) Limited, *London*
Prentice-Hall of Australia Pty. Limited, *Sydney*
Prentice-Hall Canada Inc., *Toronto*
Prentice-Hall Hispanoamericana, S.A., *Mexico*
Prentice-Hall of India Private Limited, *New Delhi*
Prentice-Hall of Japan, Inc., *Tokyo*
Simon & Schuster Asia Pte. Ltd., *Singapore*
Editora Prentice-Hall do Brasil, Ltda., *Rio de Janeiro*

Contents

Chapter 2 MODAL AUXILIARIES AND SIMILAR EXPRESSIONS

Chapter 3 THE PASSIVE

Chapter 4 GERUNDS AND INFINITIVES

Chapter 7   NOUN CLAUSES

Chapter 8   SHOWING RELATIONSHIPS BETWEEN IDEAS–PART I

Chapter 9 SHOWING RELATIONSHIPS BETWEEN IDEAS–PART II

Chapter 10 CONDITIONAL SENTENCES

Appendix 1: SUPPLEMENTARY GRAMMAR UNITS

UNIT A: BASIC GRAMMAR TERMINOLOGY

Appendix 2: PREPOSITION COMBINATIONS

Appendix 3: GUIDE TO CORRECTING WRITING ERRORS

INDEX

Preface

This is a reference grammar for students of English as a second or foreign language. With a minimum of terminology and a broad table of contents, it seeks to make essential grammar understandable and easily accessible. The charts are concise presentations of information that second/foreign language learners want and need to know in order to use English clearly, accurately, and communicatively.

Intended as a useful tool for students and teachers alike, the *Chartbook* can be used alone as a desk reference or in conjunction with the *Workbook*. The practices in the *Workbook* are keyed to the charts in the *Chartbook*.

In the *Workbook*, answers are given for the selfstudy practices, and there are also guided study practices for which no answers are given. The *Chartbook/Workbook* combination allows learners to study independently. Upper-level students can work through much of the grammar on their own. They can investigate and correct their usage problems, as well as expand their usage repertoire, by doing selfstudy practices in the *Workbook;* they can find answers to most of their grammar questions in the *Chartbook*. In addition, the teacher will have ample material from the *Workbook* to use in class or for specialized assignments.

Writing classes (or other courses, tutorials, or rapid reviews in which grammar is not the main focus but needs attention) may find the *Chartbook/Workbook* combination especially useful. Included in Appendix 3 is a guide for correcting writing errors.

Differences in structure usage between American and British English are noted throughout the text. The differences are few and relatively insignificant.

The *Teacher's Guide* for *Understanding and Using English Grammar* contains additional notes on many grammar points; each chart is discussed and amplified.

Acknowledgments

Writing may be a solitary endeavor, but book production involves a host of people. I am fortunate to be connected with a wonderful group of print professionals. I wish specifically to thank Janet Johnston for seeing every aspect of this project through from beginning to end — and for her indefatigable good cheer. Tina Carver, as always, has my sincerest appreciation for her publishing expertise and friendship.

I am also delighted to be able to thank in print: Sylvia Moore, Andy Martin, Gil Muller, Jerry Smith, Terry Jennings, Norman Harris, Karen Chiang, Ray Adame, Gordon Johnson, Eric Bredenberg, Ray Keating, Nancy Baxer, Barbara Barysh, Ed Stanford, Ros Herion Freese, and Don Martinetti. I welcome Shelley Hartle to the team. I also wish to express my appreciation to Ralph Caulo and Richard Snyder.

No books could have been written without the wonderful help and support of Don Azar. In addition, many thanks are due Joy Edwards, Barbara Matthies, Chelsea Parker, and R.T. Steltz.

I have great regard for fellow authors Steve Molinsky and Bill Bliss. I am fortunate to be associated with them.

My greatest appreciation is reserved for my much loved mother, Frances Schrampfer, who passed away recently, and for my father, William Schrampfer, who continues to assist me in my endeavors.

BETTY S. AZAR
Langley, Washington

CHAPTER **1**

Verb Tenses

AN OVERVIEW OF ENGLISH VERB TENSES FOLLOWS IN CHARTS 1-1 THROUGH 1-5. The diagram shown below will be used in the tense descriptions:

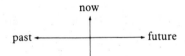

1-1 THE SIMPLE TENSES

TENSE	EXAMPLES	MEANING
SIMPLE PRESENT ✕✕✕✕✕✕✕✕✕✕✕	(a) It *snows* in Alaska. (b) I *watch* television every day.	In general, the simple present expresses events or situations that *exist always, usually, habitually*; they exist now, have existed in the past, and probably will exist in the future.
SIMPLE PAST ✕	(c) It *snowed* yesterday. (d) I *watched* television last night.	*At one particular time in the past*, this happened. It began and ended in the past.
SIMPLE FUTURE ✕	(e) It *will snow* tomorrow. (f) I *will watch* television tonight.	*At one particular time in the future*, this will happen.

1–2 THE PROGRESSIVE TENSES*

Form: **be** + **-ing** (*present participle*)

Meaning: The progressive tenses give the idea that an action is *in progress* during a particular time. The tenses say that an action *begins before*, *is in progress during*, and *continues after* another time or action.

PRESENT PROGRESSIVE	(a) He **is sleeping** right now.	He went to sleep at 10:00 tonight. It is now 11:00 and he is still asleep. His sleep began in the past, *is in progress at the present time*, and probably will continue.
PAST PROGRESSIVE	(b) He **was sleeping** when I arrived.	He went to sleep at 10:00 last night. I arrived at 11:00. He was still asleep. His sleep began before and *was in progress at a particular time in the past*. It probably continued.
FUTURE PROGRESSIVE	(c) He **will be sleeping** when we arrive.	He will go to sleep at 10:00 tomorrow night. We will arrive at 11:00. The action of sleeping will begin before we arrive and it *will be in progress at a particular time in the future*. Probably his sleep will continue.

*The progressive tenses are also called the continuous tenses: *present continuous*, *past continuous*, and *future continuous*.

Yoko **is writing** in her book. Carlos **is biting** his pencil. Wan-Ning **is scratching** his head. Ahmed **is staring** out the window.

1-3 THE PERFECT TENSES

Form: **have** + *past participle* **Meaning:** The perfect tenses all give the idea that one thing *happens before* another time or event.		
PRESENT PERFECT eat now ×————│———— (time?) │	(a) I **have** already **eaten**.	I *finished* eating some-time *before now*. The exact time is not important.
PAST PERFECT eat arrive ×——×————│———— 	(b) I **had** already **eaten** when they arrived.	First I finished eating. Later they arrived. My eating was completely *finished before another time in the past*.
FUTURE PERFECT eat arrive ————————×——×———— 	(c) I **will** already **have eaten** when they arrive.	First I will finish eating. Later they will arrive. My eating will be completely *finished before another time in the future*.

1-4 THE PERFECT PROGRESSIVE TENSES

Form: **have** + **been** + **-ing** *(present participle)* **Meaning:** The perfect progressive tenses give the idea that one event is *in progress immediately before, up to, until another time or event*. The tenses are used to express the *duration* of the first event.		
PRESENT PERFECT PROGRESSIVE ×———×————│———— └2 hrs.┘	(a) I **have been studying** for two hours.	Event in progress: studying. When? *Before now, up to now.* How long? For two hours.
PAST PERFECT PROGRESSIVE ×———×————│———— └2 hrs.┘	(b) I **had been studying** for two hours before my friend came.	Event in progress: studying. When? *Before another event in the past.* How long? For two hours.
FUTURE PERFECT PROGRESSIVE ————————×——×———— └2 hrs.┘	(c) I **will have been studying** for two hours by the time you arrive.	Event in progress: studying. When? *Before another event in the future.* How long? For two hours.

1–5 SUMMARY CHART OF VERB TENSES

SIMPLE PRESENT	PRESENT PROGRESSIVE
The world *is* round. I *study* every day.	I *am studying* right now.
SIMPLE PAST	PAST PROGRESSIVE
I *studied* last night.	I *was studying* when they came.
SIMPLE FUTURE	FUTURE PROGRESSIVE
I *will study* tomorrow.	I *will be studying* when you come.

PRESENT PERFECT	PRESENT PERFECT PROGRESSIVE
I have already *studied* Chapter One.	I *have been studying* for two hours.
PAST PERFECT	PAST PERFECT PROGRESSIVE
I *had* already *studied* Chapter One before I began to study Chapter Two.	I *had been studying* for two hours before my friends came.
FUTURE PERFECT	FUTURE PERFECT PROGRESSIVE
I *will* already *have studied* Chapter Four before I study Chapter Five.	I *will have been studying* for two hours by the time you arrive.

1–6 SPELLING OF -*ING* AND -*ED* FORMS

(1) VERBS THAT END IN -***E***	(a) hope date injure	hoping dating injuring	hoped dated injured	**-*ING* FORM**: If the word ends in -***e***, drop the -***e*** and add -***ing***.★ **-*ED* FORM**: If the word ends in -***e***, just add -***d***.
(2) VERBS THAT END IN A VOWEL AND A CONSONANT	ONE-SYLLABLE VERBS			
	(b) stop rob beg	stopping robbing begging	stopped robbed begged	*1* vowel → *2* consonants★★
	(c) rain fool dream	raining fooling dreaming	rained fooled dreamed	*2* vowels → *1* consonant
	TWO-SYLLABLE VERBS			
	(d) lísten óffer ópen	listening offering opening	listened offered opened	*1st* syllable stressed → *1* consonant
	(e) begín preférr contról	beginning preferring controlling	(began) preferred controlled	*2nd* syllable stressed → *2* consonants
(3) VERBS THAT END IN TWO CONSONANTS	(f) start fold demand	starting folding demanding	started folded demanded	If the word ends in two consonants, just add the ending.
(4) VERBS THAT END IN -***Y***	(g) enjoy pray buy	enjoying praying buying	enjoyed prayed (bought)	If -***y*** is preceded by a vowel, keep the -***y***.
	(h) study try reply	studying trying replying	studied tried replied	If -***y*** is preceded by a consonant: **-*ING* FORM**: keep the -***y***, add -***ing***. **-*ED* FORM**: change -***y*** to -***i***, add -***ed***.
(5) VERBS THAT END IN -***IE***	(i) die lie tie	dying lying tying	died lied tied	**-*ING* FORM**: Change -***ie*** to -***y***, add -***ing***. **-*ED* FORM**: Add -***d***.

★Exception: If a verb ends in -***ee***, the final -***e*** is not dropped: *seeing, agreeing, freeing.*
★★Exception: -***w*** and -***x*** are not doubled: *plow → plowed; fix → fixed.*

1–7 SIMPLE PRESENT

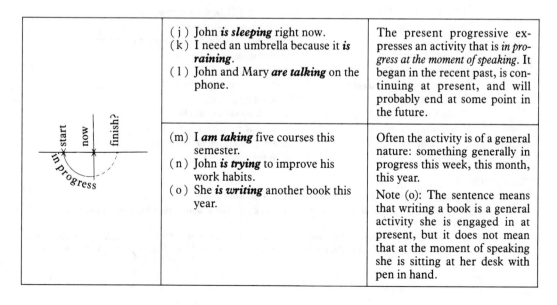

	(a) Water **consists** of hydrogen and oxygen. (b) Most animals **kill** only for food. (c) The world **is** round.	The simple present says that something was true in the past, is true in the present, and will be true in the future. It is used for *general statements of fact*.
	(d) I **study** for two hours every night. (e) My classes **begin** at nine. (f) He always **eats** a sandwich for lunch.	The simple present is used to express *habitual or everyday activity*.
	(g) I **have** only a dollar right now. (h) I **don't recognize** that man. (i) He **needs** a pen right now.	Certain verbs are not used in the progressive tenses. (See Chart 1-9.) With these verbs, the simple present may indicate a situation that exists right now, at the moment of speaking.

1–8 PRESENT PROGRESSIVE

	(j) John **is sleeping** right now. (k) I need an umbrella because it **is raining**. (l) John and Mary **are talking** on the phone.	The present progressive expresses an activity that is *in progress at the moment of speaking*. It began in the recent past, is continuing at present, and will probably end at some point in the future.
	(m) I **am taking** five courses this semester. (n) John **is trying** to improve his work habits. (o) She **is writing** another book this year.	Often the activity is of a general nature: something generally in progress this week, this month, this year. Note (o): The sentence means that writing a book is a general activity she is engaged in at present, but it does not mean that at the moment of speaking she is sitting at her desk with pen in hand.

1–9 NONPROGRESSIVE VERBS

NONPROGRESSIVE (a) Ali **knows** this grammar.	Some verbs are *nonprogressive*: they are not used in any of the progressive tenses. These verbs describe states (i.e., conditions that exist); they do not describe activities that are in progress. In (a): "Ali knows" describes a mental state that exists.
PROGRESSIVE (b) Kim **is reading** about this grammar.	COMPARE: In (b): "Kim is reading" is an activity in progress. Progressive tenses can be used with the verb **read** but not with the verb **know**.

COMMON NONPROGRESSIVE VERBS				
(1) MENTAL STATE	*know* *realize* *understand* *recognize*	*believe* *feel* *suppose* *think★*	*imagine* *doubt* *remember* *forget*	*want* *need* *prefer* *mean*
(2) EMOTIONAL STATE	*love* *like* *appreciate*	*hate* *dislike*	*fear* *envy*	*mind* *care*
(3) POSSESSION	*possess*	*have★*	*own*	*belong*
(4) SENSE PERCEPTIONS	*taste★* *smell★*	*hear* *feel★*	*see★*	
(5) OTHER EXISTING STATES	*seem* *look★* *appear★*	*cost* *owe* *weigh★*	*be★* *exist*	*consist of* *contain* *include*

*Verbs with an asterisk are also commonly used as progressive verbs, with a difference in meaning, as in the following examples:

	NONPROGRESSIVE *(existing state)*	PROGRESSIVE *(activity in progress)*
think	I **think** he is a kind man.	I **am thinking** about this grammar.
have	He **has** a car.	I **am having** trouble. She **is having** a good time.
taste	This food **tastes** good.	The chef **is tasting** the sauce.
smell	These flowers **smell** good.	Don **is smelling** the roses.
see	I **see** a butterfly. **Do** you **see** it?	The doctor **is seeing** a patient.
feel	The cat's fur **feels** soft.	Sue **is feeling** the cat's fur.
look	She **looks** cold. I'll lend her my coat.	I **am looking** out the window.
appear	He **appears** to be asleep.	The actor **is appearing** on the stage.
weigh	A piano is heavy. It **weighs** a lot.	The grocer **is weighing** the bananas.
be	I **am** hungry.	Tom **is being** foolish.**

★★COMPARE:

(a) *Bob is foolish.* = Foolishness is one of Bob's usual characteristics.

(b) *Tom is being foolish.* = Right now, at the moment of speaking, Tom is doing something that the speaker considers foolish.

The verb **be** (+ *an adjective*) is used in the progressive to describe a temporary characteristic. Very few adjectives are used with **be** in the progressive; some of the most common are: *foolish, nice, kind, lazy, careful, patient, silly, rude, polite, impolite.*

1–10 USING THE PRESENT PROGRESSIVE WITH *ALWAYS*

(a) Mary *always leaves* for school at 7:45.	In sentences referring to present time, usually the simple present is used with *always* to describe habitual or everyday activities, as in (a).
(b) Mary *is always leaving* her dirty socks on the floor for me to pick up! Who does she think I am? Her maid?	In special circumstances, a speaker may use the present progressive with *always* to complain, i.e., to express annoyance or anger, as in (b).*
(c) I *am always/forever/constantly picking* up Mary's dirty socks!	In addition to *always*, the words *forever* and *constantly* are used with the present progressive to express annoyance.

*COMPARE:
"*Mary is always leaving her dirty socks on the floor*" expresses annoyance.
"*Mary always leaves her dirty socks on the floor*" is a statement of fact in which the speaker is not necessarily expressing an attitude of annoyance. Annoyance may, however, be included in the speaker's tone of voice.

Oh no! I spilled food on my clothes again.
I'm always spilling something on my clothes.
It makes me so mad at myself!

1–11 REGULAR AND IRREGULAR VERBS

REGULAR VERBS: The simple past and past participle end in **-ed**.				English verbs have four principal parts:
SIMPLE FORM	SIMPLE PAST	PAST PARTICIPLE	PRESENT PARTICIPLE	(1) simple form (2) simple past (3) past participle (4) present participle
hope	*hoped*	*hoped*	*hoping*	
stop	*stopped*	*stopped*	*stopping*	
listen	*listened*	*listened*	*listening*	
study	*studied*	*studied*	*studying*	
start	*started*	*started*	*starting*	
IRREGULAR VERBS: The simple past and past participle do not end in **-ed**.				Some verbs have irregular past forms. Most of the irregular verbs in English are given in the following alphabetical list.
SIMPLE FORM	SIMPLE PAST	PAST PARTICIPLE	PRESENT PARTICIPLE	
break	*broke*	*broken*	*breaking*	
come	*came*	*come*	*coming*	
find	*found*	*found*	*finding*	
hit	*hit*	*hit*	*hitting*	
swim	*swam*	*swum*	*swimming*	

1–11.1 AN ALPHABETICAL LIST OF IRREGULAR VERBS

SIMPLE FORM	SIMPLE PAST	PAST PARTICIPLE	SIMPLE FORM	SIMPLE PAST	PAST PARTICIPLE
arise	arose	arisen	cling	clung	clung
be	was, were	been	come	came	come
bear	bore	borne/born	cost	cost	cost
beat	beat	beaten/beat	creep	crept	crept
become	became	become	cut	cut	cut
begin	began	begun	deal	dealt	dealt
bend	bent	bent	dig	dug	dug
bet	bet	bet★	do	did	done
bid	bid	bid	draw	drew	drawn
bind	bound	bound	eat	ate	eaten
bite	bit	bitten	fall	fell	fallen
bleed	bled	bled	feed	fed	fed
blow	blew	blown	feel	felt	felt
break	broke	broken	fight	fought	fought
breed	bred	bred	find	found	found
bring	brought	brought	fit	fit	fit★
broadcast	broadcast	broadcast	flee	fled	fled
build	built	built	fling	flung	flung
burst	burst	burst	fly	flew	flown
buy	bought	bought	forbid	forbade	forbidden
cast	cast	cast	forecast	forecast	forecast
catch	caught	caught	forget	forgot	forgotten
choose	chose	chosen	forgive	forgave	forgiven

SIMPLE FORM	SIMPLE PAST	PAST PARTICIPLE	SIMPLE FORM	SIMPLE PAST	PAST PARTICIPLE
forsake	forsook	forsaken	show	showed	shown/showed
freeze	froze	frozen	shrink	shrank/shrunk	shrunk
get	got	gotten*	shut	shut	shut
give	gave	given	sing	sang	sung
go	went	gone	sit	sat	sat
grind	ground	ground	sleep	slept	slept
grow	grew	grown	slide	slid	slid
hang	hung	hung	slit	slit	slit
have	had	had	speak	spoke	spoken
hear	heard	heard	speed	sped/speeded	sped/speeded
hide	hid	hidden	spend	spent	spent
hit	hit	hit	spin	spun	spun
hold	held	held	spit	spit/spat	spit/spat
hurt	hurt	hurt	split	split	split
keep	kept	kept	spread	spread	spread
know	knew	known	spring	sprang/sprung	sprung
lay	laid	laid	stand	stood	stood
lead	led	led	steal	stole	stolen
leave	left	left	stick	stuck	stuck
lend	lent	lent	sting	stung	stung
let	let	let	stink	stank/stunk	stunk
lie	lay	lain	strive	strove	striven
light	lit/lighted	lit/lighted	strike	struck	struck/stricken
lose	lost	lost	string	strung	strung
make	made	made	swear	swore	sworn
mean	meant	meant	sweep	swept	swept
meet	met	met	swim	swam	swum
mislay	mislaid	mislaid	swing	swung	swung
mistake	mistook	mistaken	take	took	taken
pay	paid	paid	teach	taught	taught
put	put	put	tear	tore	torn
quit	quit	quit*	tell	told	told
read	read	read	think	thought	thought
rid	rid	rid	throw	threw	thrown
ride	rode	ridden	thrust	thrust	thrust
ring	rang	rung	understand	understood	understood
rise	rose	risen	undertake	undertook	undertaken
run	ran	run	upset	upset	upset
say	said	said	wake	woke/waked	woken/waked
see	saw	seen	wear	wore	worn
seek	sought	sought	weave	wove	woven
sell	sold	sold	weep	wept	wept
send	sent	sent	win	won	won
set	set	set	wind	wound	wound
shake	shook	shaken	withdraw	withdrew	withdrawn
shed	shed	shed	wring	wrung	wrung
shine	shone/shined	shone/shined	write	wrote	written
shoot	shot	shot			

1–11.2 TROUBLESOME IRREGULAR VERBS

Differences between American English and British English:

American	British
bet-bet-bet	*bet-bet-bet* OR *bet-betted-betted*
fit-fit-fit	*fit-fitted-fitted*
get-got-gotten	*get-got-got*
quit-quit-quit	*quit-quitted-quitted*

American: *burn, dream, kneel, lean, leap, learn, smell, spell, spill, spoil* are usually regular: **burned, dreamed, kneeled, leaned, leaped,** *etc.*

British: simple past and past participle forms of these verbs can be regular but more commonly end with *-t*: **burnt, dreamt, knelt, leant, leapt, learnt, smelt, spelt, spilt, spoilt.**

Differences between transitive and intransitive verbs:

TRANSITIVE (followed by an object)	INTRANSITIVE (not followed by an object)
(a) **raise, raised, raised** Tom raised his head.	(b) **rise, rose, risen** The sun rises in the east.
(c) **set, set, set** I will set the book on the desk.	(d) **sit, sat, sat** I sit in the front row.
(e) **lay, laid, laid** I am laying the book on the desk.	(f) **lie,★ lay, lain** He is lying on his bed.
(g) **hang, hung, hung** I hung my clothes in the closet. (h) **hang, hanged, hanged** They hanged the criminal by the neck until he was dead.	

★**Lie** is a regular verb (**lie, lied**) when it means "not tell the truth": *He lied to me about his age.*

1-12 SIMPLE PAST

	(a) I **walked** to school yesterday. (b) He **lived** in Paris for ten years, but now he is living in Rome. (c) I **bought** a new car three days ago.	The simple past indicates that an activity or situation *began and ended at a particular time in the past.*
	(d) I **stood** under a tree *when it began to rain.* (e) *When she **heard** a strange noise,* she **got** up to investigate. (f) *When I **dropped** my cup,* the coffee **spilled** on my lap.	If a sentence contains **when** and has the simple past in both clauses, the action in the "**when** clause" happens first. In (d): 1st: The rain began. 2nd: I stood under a tree.

1-13 PAST PROGRESSIVE

	(g) I **was walking** down the street when it began to rain. (h) While I **was walking** down the street, it began to rain. (i) I **was standing** under a tree when it began to rain.	In (g): 1st: I was walking down the street. 2nd: It began to rain. In other words, both actions occurred at the *same* time, but *one action began earlier and was in progress when the other action occurred.*
	(j) At eight o'clock last night, I **was studying**. (k) Last year at this time, I **was attending** school.	In (j): My studying began before 8:00, was in progress at that time, and probably continued.
	(l) While I **was studying** in one room of our apartment, my roommate **was having** a party in the other room.	Sometimes the past progressive is used in both parts of a sentence when two actions are in progress simultaneously.
	(m) It **rained** this morning. (n) It **was raining** this morning.	In some cases, the simple past and the past progressive give almost the same meaning, as in (m) and (n).

(a) Kay *is studying* **in her room**. (b) Kay *is* **in her room** *studying*. (c) Jack *was* **in bed** *reading* a book when I came.	An expression of place can sometimes come between the auxiliary *be* and the *-ing* verb in a progressive tense, as in (b) and (c).

1–15 PRESENT PERFECT

(time?)	(a) They **have moved** into a new apartment. (b) **Have** you ever **visited** Mexico? (c) I **have** already **seen** that movie. (d) I **have** never **seen** snow.	The present perfect expresses the idea that something happened (or never happened) *before now, at an unspecified time in the past.* The exact time it happened is not important. If there is a specific mention of time, the simple past is used: *I saw that movie last night.*
	(e) We **have had** four tests so far this semester. (f) I **have written** my wife a letter every other day for the last two weeks. (g) I **have met** many people since I came here in June. (h) I **have flown** on an airplane many times.	The present perfect also expresses the *repetition of an activity before now*. The exact time of each repetition is not important.

	(i) I **have been** here *since seven o'clock*.
	(j) We **have been** here *for two weeks*.
	(k) I **have had** this same pair of shoes *for three years*.
	(l) I **have liked** cowboy movies ever *since I was a child*.
	(m) I **have known** him *for many years*.
		The present perfect also, when used with **for** or **since**, expresses a situation that *began in the past and continues to the present.*
		In the examples, notice the difference between **since** and **for**:
		    since + *a particular time*
		    for + *a duration of time*

NOTE: The expression *have got* can have two meanings:
   (a) I **have gotten** (British: **have got**) four letters so far this week.
   (b) I **have got** a problem.
In (a): **have gotten** (**have got**) is present perfect. In (b): **have got** is NOT present perfect. In (b) **have got** means **have**: *I've got a problem.* = *I have a problem.* The expression **have got** is common in informal spoken English. Its meaning is present; it has no past form.

1–16   PRESENT PERFECT PROGRESSIVE

	Right now I am sitting at my desk. (a) I *have been sitting* here *since* seven o'clock. (b) I *have been sitting* here *for* two hours. (c) You *have been studying for* five straight hours. Why don't you take a break? (d) It *has been raining* all day. It is still raining right now.	This tense is used to indicate the *duration* of an activity that *began in the past and continues to the present*. When the tense has this meaning, it is used with time words such as *for, since, all morning, all day, all week*.
(recently)	(e) I *have been thinking* about changing my major. (f) All of the students *have been studying* hard. Final exams start next week. (g) My back hurts, so I *have been sleeping* on the floor lately. The bed is too soft.	When the tense is used without any specific mention of time, it expresses *a general activity in progress recently, lately*.
	(h) I *have lived* here since 1985. I *have been living* here since 1985. (i) He *has worked* at the same store for ten years. He *has been working* at the same store for ten years.	With certain verbs (most notably *live, work, teach*), there is little or no difference in meaning between the two tenses when *since* or *for* is used.

1–17 PAST PERFECT

	(a) My parents **had** already **eaten** by the time I got home. (b) Until yesterday, I **had** never **heard** about it. (c) The thief simply walked in. Someone **had forgotten** to lock the door.	The past perfect expresses an activity that was *completed before another activity or time in the past.*
	(d) Sam **had** already **left** *when* we got there. (e) Sam **had left** *before* we got there. (f) Sam **left** *before* we got there. (g) *After* the guests **had** *left*, I went to bed. (h) *After* the guests *left*, I went to bed.	In (d): *First*: Sam left. *Second*: We got there.★ If either **before** or **after** is used in the sentence, the past perfect is often not necessary because the time relationship is already clear. The simple past may be used, as in (f) and (h). Note: (e) and (f) have the same meaning; (g) and (h) have the same meaning.

★COMPARE:
    Sam **left** *when* we got there. = *First*: We got there.
                                   Second: Sam left.

Millions of years ago, dinosaurs roamed the earth, but they **had become** extinct by the time humankind first **appeared**.

1-18 PAST PERFECT PROGRESSIVE

	(i) The police **had been looking** for the criminal *for* two years before they caught him. (j) The patient **had been waiting** in the emergency room *for* almost an hour before a doctor finally treated her. (k) He finally came at six o'clock. I **had been waiting** for him *since* four-thirty.	The past perfect progressive emphasizes the *duration* of an activity that was *in progress before another activity or time in the past*.
	(l) When Judy got home, her hair was still wet because she **had been swimming**. (m) Her eyes were red because she **had been crying**.	This tense also may express an activity *in progress recent to another time or activity in the past*.

1-19 SIMPLE FUTURE/*BE GOING TO*

	(a) He **will finish** his work tomorrow. (b) He **is going to finish** his work tomorrow.	**Will** or **be going to** is used to express future time.* In speech, **going to** is often pronounced "gonna."

*The use of **shall** with **I** or **we** to express future time is possible but uncommon in American English. **Shall** is used much more frequently in British than in American English.

"Stop! What are you doing?"

"I'm trying to get this piece of toast out of the toaster. It's stuck."

"Well, don't use a knife. You **will electrocute/are going to** electrocute yourself!"

"What do you suggest I do?"

"Unplug it first."

1–20 *WILL* VERSUS *BE GOING TO*

To express a PREDICTION—either *WILL* or *BE GOING TO* is used:	
(a) According to the weather report, it ***will be*** cloudy tomorrow. (b) According to the weather report, it ***is going to be*** cloudy tomorrow. (c) Be careful! You***'ll hurt*** yourself! (d) Watch out! You***'re going to*** hurt yourself!	When the speaker is making a prediction (a statement about something s/he thinks will be true or will occur in the future), either ***will*** or ***be going to*** is possible. There is no difference in meaning between (a) and (b). There is no difference in meaning between (c) and (d).
To express a PRIOR PLAN—only *BE GOING TO* is used:	
(e) A: Why did you buy this paint? B: ***I'm going to paint*** my bedroom tomorrow. (f) I talked to Bob yesterday. He is tired of taking the bus to work. He***'s going to buy*** a car. That's what he told me.	When the speaker is expressing a prior plan (something the speaker intends to do in the future because in the past s/he has made a plan or decision to do it), only ***be going to*** is used.* In (e): Speaker B has made a prior plan. She decided to paint her bedroom last week. She intends to paint her bedroom tomorrow. In (f): The speaker knows Bob's intention to buy a car. Bob made the decision in the past and he intends to act on this decision in the future. ***Will*** is not appropriate in (e) and (f).
To express WILLINGNESS—only *WILL* is used:	

(g) A: The phone's ringing.
      B: I***'ll get*** it.
 	
 (h) A: I don't understand this problem.
      B: Ask your teacher about it. She***'ll help*** you.
	In (g): Speaker B is saying: "I am willing, I am happy to get the phone." He is not making a prediction. He has made no prior plan to answer the phone. He is, instead, volunteering to answer the phone and uses ***will*** to show his willingness.
	
	 In (h): Speaker B feels sure about the teacher's willingness to help.
	 Be going to is not appropriate in (g) and (h).

*COMPARE:

     Situation 1: *A: Are you busy this evening?*
                 B: Yes. ***I'm going to meet*** *Jack at the library at seven. We****'re going to study*** *together.*
In situation 1, only ***be going to*** is possible. The speaker has a prior plan, so he uses ***be going to***.

     Situation 2: *A: Are you busy this evening?*
                 *B: Well, I really haven't made any plans. I'****ll eat****/I'****m going to eat*** *dinner, of course. And then I'****ll***
                     probably watch*/I'****m probably going to watch*** *TV for a little while.*
In situation 2, either ***will*** or ***be going to*** is possible. Speaker B has not planned his evening. He is "predicting" his evening (rather than stating any prior plans), so he may use either ***will*** or ***be going to***.

1-21 EXPRESSING THE FUTURE IN TIME CLAUSES

(a) Bob will come soon. *When Bob **comes**,* we will see him. (b) Linda is going to leave soon. *Before she **leaves**,* she is going to finish her work. (c) I will get home at 5:30. *After **I get** home,* I will eat dinner. (d) The taxi will arrive soon. *As soon as it **arrives**,* we'll be able to leave for the airport. (e) They are going to come soon. I'll wait here *until they **come**.*	In (a): "When Bob comes" is a time clause.* ***when** + subject + verb = a time clause* **Will** or **be going to** is NOT used in a time clause. The meaning of the clause is future, but the simple present tense is used.

	A time clause begins with such words as **when, before, after, as soon as, until** and includes a subject and a verb. The time clause can come either at the beginning of the sentence or in the second part of the sentence:
	    When he comes, we'll see him.
	    OR:
	    We'll see him *when he comes.*

(f) I will go to bed *after **I finish** my work.* (g) I will go to bed *after **I have finished** my work.*	Occasionally, the present perfect is used in a time clause, as in (g). Examples (f) and (g) have the same meaning. The present perfect stresses the completion of the act in the time clause before the other act occurs in the future.

*A "time clause" is an adverb clause. See Chart 8-5 for more information.

1-22 USING THE PRESENT PROGRESSIVE AND THE SIMPLE PRESENT TO EXPRESS FUTURE TIME

PRESENT PROGRESSIVE (a) My wife has an appointment with a doctor. She **is seeing** Dr. North *next Tuesday.* (b) Sam has already made his plans. He **is leaving** *at noon tomorrow.* (c) A: What are you going to do this afternoon? B: *After lunch* I **am meeting** a friend of mine. We **are going** shopping. Would you like to come along?	The present progressive may be used to express future time when the idea of the sentence concerns a planned event or definite intention. (COMPARE: A verb such as *rain* is not used in the present progressive to indicate future time because rain is not a planned event.) A future meaning for the present progressive tense is indicated either by future time words in the sentence or by the context.
SIMPLE PRESENT (d) The museum **opens** *at ten tomorrow morning.* (e) Classes **begin** *next week.* (f) John's plane **arrives** *at 6:05 P.M. next Monday.*	The simple present can also be used to express future time in sentences that concern events that are on a definite schedule or timetable. These sentences usually contain future time words. Only a few verbs are used in this way: e.g., *open, close, begin, end, start, finish, arrive, leave, come, return.*

1–23 FUTURE PROGRESSIVE

	(a) I will begin to study at seven. You will come at eight. I *will be studying* when you come. (b) Right now I am sitting in class. At this same time tomorrow, I *will be sitting* in class.	The future progressive expresses an activity that will be *in progress at a time in the future.*
	(c) Don't call me at nine because I won't be home. I *am going to be studying* at the library.	The progressive form of *be going to*: *be going to + be + -ing*
	(d) Don't get impatient. She *will be coming* soon. (e) Don't get impatient. She *will come* soon.	Sometimes there is little or no difference between the future progressive and the simple future, especially when the future event will occur at an indefinite time in the future, as in (d) and (e).

I'm leaving for Florida tomorrow. Two days from now I *will be lying* on the beach in the sun.

1–24 FUTURE PERFECT

	(a) I will graduate in June. I will see you in July. By the next time I see you, I *will have graduated*. (b) I *will have finished* my homework by the time I go out on a date tonight.	The future perfect expresses an activity that will be *completed before another time or event in the future.* (Notice in the examples: *by the time* introduces a time clause; the simple present is used in a time clause.)

1-25 FUTURE PERFECT PROGRESSIVE

	(c) I will go to bed at ten P.M. He will get home at midnight. At midnight I will be sleeping. I **_will have been sleeping_** for two hours by the time he gets home.	The future perfect progressive emphasizes the *duration* of an activity that will be *in progress before another time or event in the future*.
	(d) When Professor Jones retires next month, he **_will have taught_** for 45 years. (e) When Professor Jones retires next month, he **_will have been teaching_** for 45 years.	Sometimes the future perfect and the future perfect progressive give the same meaning, as in (d) and (e). Also, notice that the activity expressed by either of these two tenses may begin in the past.

CHAPTER *2*

Modal Auxiliaries and Similar Expressions

2–1 INTRODUCTION

The modal auxiliaries in English are: ***can***, ***could***, ***had better***, ***may***, ***might***, ***must***, ***ought to***, ***shall***, ***should***, ***will***, ***would***.

Modal auxiliaries generally express a speaker's attitudes, or "moods." For example, modals can express that a speaker feels something is necessary, advisable, permissible, possible, or probable; and, in addition, they can convey the strength of these attitudes.

Each modal has more than one meaning or use. (See Chart 2-23.)

(a) MODAL AUXILIARIES	Modals do not take a final **-s**, even when the subject is *he*, *she*, or *it*. CORRECT: ***He can*** *do it.* *INCORRECT: He cans do it.*

I
We
You
They +
He
She
It
 	
can *do* it.
could *do* it.
had better *do* it.
may *do* it.
might *do* it.
must *do* it.
ought to *do* it.
shall *do* it.
should *do* it.
will *do* it.
would *do* it.
	Modals are followed immediately by the simple form of a verb.
	     CORRECT: *He* ***can do*** *it.*
	INCORRECT: He can to do it./He can does it./He can did it.
	The only exception is ***ought***, which is followed by an infinitive (***to*** + the simple form of a verb).
	     CORRECT: *She* ***ought to go*** *to the meeting.*

(b) SIMILAR EXPRESSIONS ***be able to*** *do* it ***be going to*** *do* it ***be supposed to*** *do* it ***be to*** *do* it ***have to*** *do* it ***have got to*** *do* it ***used to*** *do* it	In (b) is a list of some common expressions whose meanings are similar to those of some of the modal auxiliaries. For example, ***be able to*** is similar to ***can***; ***be going to*** is similar to ***will***. An infinitive (***to*** + the simple form of a verb) is used in these similar expressions.

2–2 POLITE REQUESTS WITH "I" AS THE SUBJECT

MAY I COULD I	(a) *May I* (please) *borrow* your pen? (b) *Could I borrow* your pen (please)?	*May I* and *could I* are used to request permission. They are equally polite.★ Note in (b): In a polite request, *could* has a present or future meaning, not a past meaning.
CAN I	(c) *Can I borrow* your pen?	*Can I* is used informally to request permission, especially if the speaker is talking to someone s/he knows fairly well. *Can I* is usually not considered as polite as *may I* or *could I*.
	TYPICAL RESPONSES: Certainly. Yes, certainly. Of course. Yes, of course. Sure. (*informal*)	Often the response to a polite request consists of an action, a nod or shake of the head, or a simple "uh-huh."

★Might is also possible: *Might I borrow your pen*. *Might I* is quite formal and polite; it is used much less frequently than *may I* or *could I*.

2–3 POLITE REQUESTS WITH "YOU" AS THE SUBJECT

WOULD YOU WILL YOU	(a) *Would you pass* the salt (please)? (b) *Will you* (please) *pass* the salt?	The meaning of *would you* and *will you* in a polite request is the same. *Would you* is more common and is often considered more polite. The degree of politeness, however, is often determined by the speaker's tone of voice.
COULD YOU	(c) *Could you pass* the salt?	Basically, *could you* and *would you* have the same meaning. The difference is slight: *would you* = *Do you want to do this please?* *could you* = *Do you want to do this please, and is it possible for you to do this?* *Could you* and *would you* are equally polite.
CAN YOU	(d) *Can you pass* the salt?	*Can you* is often used informally. It usually sounds less polite than *could you* or *would you*.
	TYPICAL RESPONSES: Yes, I'd (I would) be happy to. Yes, I'd be glad to. Certainly. Sure. (*informal*)	A person usually responds in the affirmative to a polite request. If a negative response is necessary, a person might begin by saying, "I'd like to, but . . ." (e.g., "I'd like to pass the salt, but I can't reach it. I'll ask Tom to pass it to you.").

2–4 POLITE REQUESTS WITH *WOULD YOU MIND*

ASKING PERMISSION (a) *Would you mind **if I closed** the window?* (b) *Would you mind **if I used** the phone?*	Notice in (a): ***would you mind if I*** is followed by the simple past.* The meaning in (a): *May I close the window? Is it all right if I close the window? Will it cause you any trouble or discomfort if I close the window?*
TYPICAL RESPONSES No. Not at all. No, of course not. No, that would be fine.	Another typical response might be "unh-unh," meaning *no*.
ASKING SOMEONE ELSE TO DO SOMETHING (c) *Would you mind **closing** the window?* (d) *Excuse me? Would you mind **repeating** that?*	Notice in (c): ***would you mind*** is followed by ***-ing*** (a gerund). The meaning in (c): *I don't want to cause you any trouble, but would you please close the window? Would that cause you any inconvenience?*
TYPICAL RESPONSES No. I'd be happy to. Not at all. I'd be glad to.	

*Sometimes in informal spoken English, the simple present is used: *Would you mind if I close the window?* (Note: The simple past does not refer to past time after *would you mind*; it refers to present or future time. See Chart 10-3 for more information.)

2–5 USING IMPERATIVE SENTENCES TO MAKE POLITE REQUESTS

(a) ***Shut*** the door. (b) ***Be*** on time. (c) ***Don't shut*** the door. (d) ***Don't be*** late.	An imperative sentence has an understood subject (*you*), and the verb (*e.g., shut*) is in the simple form. *Shut the door.* = (*You*) *shut the door. Be on time.* = (*You*) *be on time.* In the negative, ***don't*** precedes the simple form of the verb.
(e) ***Turn*** right at the corner. (f) ***Shut*** the door. (g) ***Please shut*** the door. ***Shut*** the door, ***please***.	An imperative sentence can be used to give directions, as in (e). An imperative sentence can be used to give an order, as in (f). It can also be used to make a polite request, as in (g), when the word ***please*** is added.*

*Sometimes ***would you/could you*** is added as a tag question (almost as an afterthought) to turn an imperative into a polite request; e.g., *Shut the door, would/could you?* Sometimes, usually in a formal situation, ***won't you*** is added to an imperative as a tag question to make a polite request; e.g., *Have a seat, won't you?* (See Appendix 1, Chart B-4 for information about tag questions.)

2-6 EXPRESSING NECESSITY: *MUST, HAVE TO, HAVE GOT TO*

(a) All applicants *must take* an entrance exam.	*Must* and *have to* both express necessity.
(b) All applicants *have to take* an entrance exam.	In (a) and (b): It is necessary for every applicant to take an entrance exam. There is no other choice. The exam is required.
(c) I'm looking for Sue. I *have to talk* to her about our lunch date tomorrow. I can't meet her for lunch because I *have to go* to a business meeting at 1:00. (d) Where's Sue? I *must talk* to her right away. I have an urgent message for her.	In everyday statements of necessity, *have to* is used more commonly than *must*. *Must* is usually stronger than *have to* and can indicate urgency or stress importance. In (c): The speaker is simply saying, "I need to do this and I need to do that." In (d): The speaker is strongly saying, "This is very important!"
(e) I *have to* ("hafta") be home by eight. (f) He *has to* ("hasta") go to a meeting tonight.	Note: *have to* is usually pronounced "hafta"; *has to* is usually pronounced "hasta."
(g) I *have got to go* now. I have a class in ten minutes. (h) I *have to go* now. I have a class in ten minutes.	*Have got to* also expresses the idea of necessity: (g) and (h) have the same meaning. *Have got to* is informal and is used primarily in spoken English. *Have to* is used in both formal and informal English.
(i) I *have got to go* ("I've gotta go/I gotta go") now.	Usual pronunciation of *got to* is "gotta." Sometimes *have* is dropped in speech: "I gotta do it."
(j) PRESENT or FUTURE I *have to/have got to/must study* tonight. (k) PAST: I *had to study* last night.	The idea of past necessity is expressed by *had to*. There is no other past form for *must* (when it means necessity) or *have got to*.

2-7 LACK OF NECESSITY AND PROHIBITION: *HAVE TO* AND *MUST* IN THE NEGATIVE

LACK OF NECESSITY (a) Tomorrow is a holiday. We *don't have to go* to class. (b) I can hear you. You *don't have to shout*.*	When used in the negative, *must* and *have to* have different meanings.
	do not have to = *lack of necessity*. In (a): It is not necessary for us to go to class tomorrow because there is a holiday.
PROHIBITION (c) You *must not look* in the closet. Your birthday present is hidden there. (d) You *must not tell* anyone my secret. Do you promise?	*must not* = *prohibition* (DO NOT DO THIS!) In (c): Do not look in the closet. I forbid it. Looking in the closet is prohibited.
	Negative contraction: *mustn't*. (The first "t" is not pronounced: "muss-ənt.")

*Lack of necessity may also be expressed by *need not* + *the simple form of a verb: You *needn't shout*. The use of *needn't* as an auxiliary is chiefly British other than when it is used in certain common expressions such as "You needn't worry."

2-8 ADVISABILITY: *SHOULD, OUGHT TO, HAD BETTER*

(a) You ***should study*** harder. You ***ought to study*** harder. (b) Drivers ***should obey*** the speed limit. Drivers ***ought to obey*** the speed limit.	***Should*** and ***ought to*** have the same meaning: they express advisability. The meaning ranges in strength from a suggestion (''This is a good idea.'') to a statement about responsibility or duty (''This is a very important thing to do.''). In (a): ''This is a good idea. This is my advice.'' In (b): ''This is an important responsibility.''
(c) You ***shouldn't leave*** your keys in the car.	Negative contraction: ***shouldn't***.*
(d) I ***ought to*** (''otta'') ***study*** tonight, but I think I'll watch TV instead.	***Ought to*** is sometimes pronounced ''otta'' in informal speaking.
(e) The gas tank is almost empty. We ***had better stop*** at the next service station. (f) You ***had better take*** care of that cut on your hand soon, or it will get infected.	In meaning, ***had better*** is close to ***should/ought to***, but ***had better*** is usually stronger. Often ***had better*** implies a warning or a threat of possible bad consequences. In (e): If we don't stop at a service station, there will be a bad result. We will run out of gas. Notes: ***Had better*** has a present or future meaning. It is followed by the simple form of a verb. It is more common in speaking than writing.
(g) You***'d better*** take care of it. (h) You ***better*** take care of it. (i) You***'d better not*** be late.	Contraction: ***'d better***, as in (g). Sometimes in speaking, ***had*** is dropped, as in (h). Negative form: ***had better*** + ***not***.

*****Ought to*** is not commonly used in the negative. If it is used in the negative, the ***to*** is often dropped: *You* ***oughtn't (to) leave*** *your keys in the car.*

''I'm cold.''

''You ***should put*** on a sweater.''
''You ***ought to drink*** some hot tea.''
''You ***had better go*** inside and ***get*** warm.''

2–9 THE PAST FORM OF *SHOULD*

(a) I had a test this morning. I didn't do well on the test because I didn't study for it last night. I **should have studied** last night. (b) You were supposed to be here at 10 P.M., but you didn't come until midnight. We were worried about you. You **should have called** us. (You did not call.)	Past form: **should have** + *past participle.*★ In (a): "I should have studied" means that studying was a good idea, but I didn't do it. I made a mistake. Usual pronunciation of **should have**: "should-of" or "shoulda."
(c) I hurt my back. I **should not have carried** that heavy box up two flights of stairs. (I carried the box and now I am sorry.) (d) We went to the movie, but it was a bad movie. We wasted our time and money. We **should not have gone** to the movie.	In (c): "I should not have carried" means that I carried something, but it turned out to be a bad idea. I made a mistake. Usual pronunciation of **should not have**: "shouldn't-of" or "shouldn't'a."

★The past form of **ought to** is **ought to have** + *past participle*. (*I ought to have studied*.) It has the same meaning as the past form of **should**. In the past, **should** is used more commonly than **ought to**. **Had better** is only rarely used in a past form (e.g., *He **had better have taken** care of it*.) and usually only in speaking, not writing.

2–10 EXPECTATIONS: *BE SUPPOSED TO* AND *BE TO*

(a) The game **is supposed to begin** at 10:00. (b) The game **is to begin** at 10:00. (c) The committee **is supposed to meet** tomorrow. (d) The committee **is to meet** tomorrow.	**Be supposed to** and **be to** (a form of **be** followed immediately by an infinitive, e.g., *is to begin*) express the idea that someone (I, we, they, the teacher, lots of people, my father, etc.) expects something to happen. **Be supposed to** and **be to** often express expectations about scheduled events or correct procedures. In (a) and (b): The speaker expects the game to begin at 10:00 because that is the schedule. **Be to** is stronger, more definite, than **be supposed to**.
COMPARE: (e) I **should go** to the meeting. I can get some information if I go. Going to the meeting is a good idea.	**Be supposed to** and **be to** also express expectations about behavior; often they give the idea that someone expects a particular person to do something.
(f) I **am supposed to go** to the meeting. My boss told me that he wants me to attend.	**Be supposed to** is close in meaning to **should**, but **be supposed to**, as in (f), gives the idea that someone else expects (requests or requires) this behavior.
COMPARE: (g) I **must be** at the meeting. The meeting can't occur without me because I'm the only one who has certain information.	**Be to** is close in meaning to **must**, but **be to**, as in (h), includes the idea that someone else strongly expects (demands or orders) this behavior.
(h) I **am to be** at the meeting. My boss ordered me to be there. He will accept no excuses.	**Be to** is used to state strong expectations: e.g., rules, laws, instructions, demands, orders.

2–11 MAKING SUGGESTIONS: *LET'S, WHY DON'T, SHALL I/WE*

(a) **Let's go** to a movie. (b) **Let's not go** to a movie. **Let's stay** home instead.	**Let's** = **let us**. **Let's** is followed by the simple form of a verb. Negative form: **let's** + **not** + *simple verb*. The meaning of **let's**: "I have a suggestion for us."
(c) **Why don't we go** to a movie? (d) **Why don't you come** around seven? (e) **Why don't I give** Mary a call?	**Why don't** is used primarily in spoken English to make a friendly suggestion. In (c): **why don't we go** = **let's go**. In (d): I suggest that you come around seven. In (e): Should I give Mary a call? Do you agree with my suggestion?
(f) **Shall I open** the window? Is that okay with you? (g) **Shall we leave** at two? Is that okay? (h) Let's go, **shall we**? (i) Let's go, **okay**?	When **shall** is used with "I" or "we" in a question, the speaker is usually making a suggestion and asking another person if s/he agrees with this suggestion. Sometimes "shall we?" is used as a tag question after **let's**. More informally, "okay?" is used as a tag question, as in (i).

2–12 MAKING SUGGESTIONS: *COULD*

--*What should we do tomorrow?* (a) Why don't we go on a picnic? (b) We **could go** on a picnic.	**Could** can be used to make suggestions. (b) is similar to (a) in meaning; i.e., the speaker is suggesting a picnic.
--*I'm having trouble in math class.* (c) You **should talk** to your teacher.	**Should** gives definite advice. In (c), the speaker is saying: "I believe it is important for you to do this. This is what I recommend."
--*I'm having trouble in math class.* (d) You **could talk** to your teacher. Or you **could ask** Ann to help you with your math lessons. Or I **could try** to help you.	**Could** offers suggestions or possibilities. In (d), the speaker is saying: "I have some possible suggestions for you. It is possible to do this. Or it is possible to do that."★
--*I failed my math class.* (e) You **should have talked** to your teacher and gotten some help from her during the term.	**Should have** gives "hindsight advice."★★ In (e), the speaker is saying: "It was important for you to talk to the teacher, but you didn't do it. You made a mistake."
--*I failed my math class.* (f) You **could have talked** to your teacher. Or you **could have asked** Ann to help you with your math. Or I **could have tried** to help you.	**Could have** offers "hindsight possibilities."★★ In (f), the speaker is saying: "You had the chance to do this or that. It was possible for this or that to happen. You missed some good opportunities."

★***Might*** (but not ***may***) can also be used to make suggestions (*You **might talk** to your teacher.*), but the use of **could** is more common.
★★"Hindsight" refers to looking at something after it happens.

--Why isn't John in class? **100% sure**: He *is* sick. **95% sure**: He *must be* sick. He *may be* sick. **less than 50% sure**: He *might be* sick. He *could be* sick.	"Degree of certainty" refers to how sure we are—what we think the chances are—that something is true. If we are sure something is true in the present, we don't need to use a modal. For example, if I say, "John is sick," I am sure; I am stating a fact that I am sure is true. My degree of certainty is 100%.
--Why isn't John in class? (a) He *must be* sick. (Usually he is in class every day, but when I saw him last night, he wasn't feeling good. So my best guess is that he is sick today. I can't think of another possibility.)	**Must** is used to express a strong degree of certainty about a present situation, but the degree of certainty is still less than 100%.
	In (a): The speaker is saying: "Probably John is sick. I have evidence to make me believe that he is sick. That is my logical conclusion, but I do not know for certain."
--Why isn't John in class? (b) He *may be* sick.	**May**, **might**, and **could** are used to express a weak degree of certainty.
(c) He *might be* sick. (d) He *could be* sick. (I don't really know. He may be at home watching TV. He might be at the library. He could be out of town.)	In (b), (c), and (d): The speaker is saying: "Perhaps, maybe,* possibly John is sick. I am only making a guess. I can think of other possibilities." (b), (c), and (d) have the same meaning.

*__Maybe__ (spelled as one word) is an adverb: __Maybe__ *he is sick*. __May be__ (spelled as two words) is a verb form: *He __may be__ sick*.

"You're coughing and sneezing, blowing your nose, and running a fever. You **must feel** terrible."
"I do."

2-14   DEGREES OF CERTAINTY: PRESENT TIME NEGATIVE

100% sure:	Sam *isn't* hungry.
99% sure:	Sam *couldn't be* hungry. Sam *can't be* hungry.
95% sure:	Sam *must not be* hungry.
less than 50% sure:	Sam *may not be* hungry. Sam *might not be* hungry.

(a) Sam doesn't want anything to eat. He *isn't* hungry. He told me his stomach is full. He says he isn't hungry. I believe him.	In (a): The speaker is sure that Sam is not hungry.
(b) Sam *couldn't/can't be* hungry! That's impossible! I just saw him eat a huge meal. He has already eaten enough to fill two grown men. Did he really say he'd like something to eat? I don't believe it.	In (b): The speaker believes that there is no possibility that Sam is hungry (but the speaker is not 100% sure). Notice the negative use: *couldn't* and *can't* forcefully express the idea that the speaker believes something is impossible.
(c) Sam isn't eating his food. He *must not be* hungry. That's the only reason I can think of.	In (c): The speaker is expressing a logical conclusion, a "best guess."
(d) I don't know why Sam isn't eating his food. He *may/might not be* hungry right now. Or maybe he doesn't feel well. Or perhaps he ate just before he got here. Who knows?	In (d): The speaker uses *may not/might not* to mention a possibility.

"I think there's a dragon on top of the house, Dad!"
"Son, it *couldn't be* a dragon. We don't have any dragons
around here. They exist only in story books."

2–15 DEGREES OF CERTAINTY: PAST TIME

PAST TIME: AFFIRMATIVE	In (a): The speaker is sure.
--Why wasn't Mary in class?	In (b): The speaker is making a logical conclusion; e.g., "I saw Mary yesterday and found out that she was sick. I assume that is the reason why she was absent. I can't think of any other good reason."
(a) **100%:** She *was* sick.	
(b) **95%:** She *must have been* sick.	
She *may have been* sick.	
(c) **less than 50%:** She *might have been* sick. She *could have been* sick.	In (c): The speaker is mentioning one possibility.
PAST TIME: NEGATIVE	
(d) **100%:** Sam *wasn't* hungry.	In (d): The speaker is sure.
(e) **99%:** Sam *couldn't have been* hungry. Sam *can't have been* hungry.	In (e): The speaker believes that it is impossible for Sam to have been hungry.
(f) **95%:** Sam *must not have been* hungry.	In (f): The speaker is making a logical conclusion.
(g) **less than 50%:** Sam *may not have been* hungry. Sam *might not have been* hungry.	In (g): The speaker is mentioning one possibility.

2–16 DEGREES OF CERTAINTY: FUTURE TIME★

100% sure:	Kay *will do* well on the test.	→ *(The speaker feels sure.)*
90% sure:	She *should do* well on the test. She *ought to do* well on the test.	→ *(The speaker is almost sure.)*
less than 50% sure:	She *may do* well on the test. She *might do* well on the test. She *could do* well on the test.	→ *(The speaker is guessing.)*

(a) Kay has been studying hard. She *should do/ought to do* well on the test tomorrow.	*Should/ought to* can be used to express expectations about future events. In (a): The speaker is saying, "Kay will probably do well on the test. I expect her to do well. That is what I think will happen."
(b) I wonder why Sue hasn't written us. We *should have heard/ought to have heard* from her last week.	The past form of *should/ought to* is used to mean that the speaker expected something that did not occur.

★COMPARE: *Must* expresses a strong degree of certainty about a *present* situation. (See Chart 2-13.) *Should* and *ought to* express a fairly strong degree of certainty about a *future* situation. *Will* indicates that there is no doubt in the speaker's mind about a *future* event.

2-17 PROGRESSIVE FORMS OF MODALS

(a) Let's just knock on the door lightly. Tom **may be sleeping**. (*right now*) (b) All of the lights in Ann's room are turned off. She **must be sleeping**. (*right now*)	Progressive form, present time: *modal* + **be** + **-ing**. Meaning: *in progress right now.*
(c) Sue wasn't at home last night when we went to visit her. She **might have been studying** at the library. (d) Al wasn't at home last night. He has a lot of exams coming up soon, and he is also working on a term paper. He **must have been studying** at the library.	Progressive form, past time: *modal* + **have been** + **-ing**. Meaning: *in progress at a time in the past.*

2-18 USING *USED TO* (HABITUAL PAST) AND *BE USED TO*

(a) Jack **used to live** in Chicago.	In (a): At a time in the past, Jack lived in Chicago, but he does not live in Chicago now. **Used to** expresses a habit, activity, or situation that existed in the past but which no longer exists.
(b) Mary **is used to** cold weather. (c) Mary **is accustomed to** cold weather.	**Be used to** means **be accustomed to**. (b) and (c) have the same meaning: Living in a cold climate is usual and normal to Mary. Cold weather, snow, and ice do not seem strange to her.
COMPARE: (d) Jack **used to live** in Chicago. (e) Mary **is used to living** in a cold climate. She **is accustomed to living** there.	To express habitual past, **used** is followed by an infinitive, e.g., **to live** as in (d). **Be used to** and **be accustomed to** are followed by an **-ing** verb form (a gerund*), as in (e).
(f) Bob moved to Alaska. After a while he **got used to/got accustomed to** living in a cold climate.	In the expressions **get used to** and **get accustomed to**, **get** means **become**.

*See Chart 4-2, *Using Gerunds as the Objects of Prepositions.*

2–19 USING *WOULD* TO EXPRESS A REPEATED ACTION IN THE PAST

(a) When I was a child, my father **would read** me a story at night before bed. (b) When I was a child, my father **used to read** me a story at night before bed.	***Would*** can be used to express *an action* that was repeated regularly in the past. When ***would*** is used to express this idea, it has the same meaning as ***used to*** (*habitual past*). (a) and (b) have the same meaning.
(c) I **used to live** in California. He **used to be** a Boy Scout. They **used to have** a Ford.	When ***used to*** expresses *a situation* that existed in the past, as in (c), ***would*** may not be used as an alternative. ***Would*** is used only for regularly repeated *actions* in the past.

When I was a child, I **would take** a flashlight to bed with me so that
I could read comic books without my parents' knowing about it.

2–20 EXPRESSING PREFERENCE: *WOULD RATHER*

(a) I **would rather go** to a movie tonight *than* **study** grammar. (b) **I'd rather study** history *than* (**study**) biology.	***Would rather*** expresses preference. In (a): Notice that the simple form of a verb follows both ***would rather*** and ***than***. In (b): If the verb is the same, it does not have to be repeated after ***than***.
--*How much do you weigh?* (c) **I'd rather not tell** you.	Contraction: ***I would*** = ***I'd***. Negative form: ***would rather*** + ***not***.
(d) The movie was okay, but I **would rather have gone** to the concert last night.	The past form: ***would rather have*** + *past participle*. Usual pronunciation: "I'd rather-of."
(e) **I'd rather be lying** on a beach in Florida *than* (**be**) **sitting** in class right now.	Progressive form: ***would rather*** + ***be*** + ***-ing***.

2–21 USING *CAN* AND *BE ABLE TO*

(a) Tom is strong. He **can lift** that heavy box. (b) I **can play** the piano. I've taken lessons for many years. (c) You **can see** fish at an aquarium. (d) That race car **can go** very fast.	**Can** usually expresses the idea that something is possible because certain characteristics or conditions exist. **Can** combines the ideas of *possibility* and *ability*. In (a): It is possible for Tom to lift that box because he is strong. In (b): It is possible for me to play the piano because I have acquired that ability. In (c): It is possible to see fish at an aquarium because an aquarium has fish. In (d): It is possible for that car to go fast because of its special characteristics.
(e) Dogs can bark, but they **cannot/can't talk**.	Negative form: **cannot** or **can't**. (Also possible, but not as common: **can not**, written as two words.)
COMPARE: (f) I **can walk** to school. It's not far. (g) I **may walk** to school. Or I may take the bus.	In (f): I can walk to school because certain conditions exist. In (g): I am less than 50% certain that I will walk to school.
COMPARE: (h) I'm not quite ready to go, but you **can leave** if you're in a hurry. I'll meet you later. (i) When you finish the test, you **may leave**.	**Can** is also used to give permission. In giving permission, **can** is usually used in informal situations, as in (h); **may** is usually used in formal situations, as in (i).
COMPARE: (j) Tom **can lift** that box. (k) *Uncommon:* Tom **is able to lift** that box. (l) Ann **will be able to lift** that box. Bob **may be able to lift** that box. Sue **should be able to lift** that box. Jim **used to be able to lift** that box.	The use of **be able to** in the simple present (*am/is/are able to*) is uncommon (but possible). **Be able to** is more commonly used in combination with other auxiliaries, as in (l).

2-22 PAST ABILITY: *COULD*

(a) When I was younger, I **could run** fast. (*Probable meaning*: I used to be able to run fast, but now I can't run fast.)	In affirmative sentences about past ability, **could** usually means "used to be able to." The use of **could** usually indicates that the ability existed in the past but does not exist now.
(b) Tom has started an exercise program. He **was able to run** two miles yesterday without stopping or slowing down.	If the speaker is talking about an ability to perform an act at one particular time in the past, **was/were able to** can be used in affirmative sentences but not **could**. **Could** is not appropriate in (b).
--Did you read the news about the mountain climbers? (c) INCORRECT: *They* **could reach** *the top of Mt. Everest yesterday.* (d) CORRECT: They **were able to reach** the top yesterday. They **managed to reach** the top yesterday. They **reached** the top yesterday.	Note that (c) is incorrect. Instead of **could**, the speaker needs to use **were able to**, **managed to**, or *the simple past*.
(e) They *couldn't reach/weren't able to reach* the top yesterday. (f) Tom *couldn't run/wasn't able to run* five miles yesterday.	In negative sentences, there is no difference between using **could** and **was/were able to**.

2-23 SUMMARY CHART OF MODALS AND SIMILAR EXPRESSIONS

AUXILIARY	USES	PRESENT/FUTURE	PAST
may	(1) polite request	**May** I **borrow** your pen?	
	(2) formal permission	You **may leave** the room.	
	(3) less than 50% certainty	--Where's John? He **may be** at the library.	He **may have been** at the library.
might	(1) less than 50% certainty	--Where's John? He **might be** at the library.	He **might have been** at the library.
	(2) polite request (*rare*)	**Might** I **borrow** your pen?	

(continued)

AUXILIARY	USES	PRESENT/FUTURE	PAST
should	(1) advisability	I ***should study*** tonight.	I ***should have studied*** last night
	(2) 90% certainty	She ***should do*** well on the test. (*future only, not present*)	She ***should have done*** well on the test.
ought to	(1) advisability	I ***ought to study*** tonight.	I ***ought to have studied*** last night.
	(2) 90% certainty	She ***ought to do*** well on the test. (*future only, not present*)	She ***ought to have done*** well on the test.
had better	(1) advisability with threat of bad result	You ***had better be*** on time, or we will leave without you.	(*past form uncommon*)
be supposed to	(1) expectation	Class ***is supposed to begin*** at 10.	Class ***was supposed to begin*** at 10.
be to	(1) strong expectation	You ***are to be*** here at 9:00.	You ***were to be*** here at 9:00.
must	(1) strong necessity	I ***must go*** to class today.	I ***had to go*** to class yesterday.
	(2) prohibition (*negative*)	You ***must not*** open that door.	
	(3) 95% certainty	Mary isn't in class. She ***must be*** sick. (*present only*)	Mary ***must have been*** sick yesterday.
have to	(1) necessity	I ***have to go*** to class today.	I ***had to go*** to class yesterday.
	(2) lack of necessity (*negative*)	I ***don't have to go*** to class today.	I ***didn't have to go*** to class yesterday.
have got to	(1) necessity	I ***have got to go*** to class today.	I ***had to go*** to class yesterday.
will	(1) 100% certainty	He ***will be*** here at 6:00. (*future only*)	
	(2) willingness	--The phone's ringing. ***I'll get*** it.	
	(3) polite request	***Will*** you please ***pass*** the salt?	
be going to	(1) 100% certainty	He ***is going to be*** here at 6:00. (*future only*)	
	(2) definite plan	***I'm going to paint*** my bedroom. (*future only*)	I ***was going to paint*** my room, but I didn't have time.

AUXILIARY	USES	PRESENT/FUTURE	PAST
can	(1) ability/possibility	I *can run* fast.	I *could run* fast when I was a child, but now I can't.
	(2) informal permission	You *can use* my car tomorrow.	
	(3) informal polite request	*Can* I *borrow* your pen?	
	(4) impossibility (*negative only*)	That *can't be* true!	That *can't have been* true!
could	(1) past ability		I *could run* fast when I was a child.
	(2) polite request	*Could* I *borrow* your pen? *Could* you *help* me?	
	(3) suggestion	--I need help in math. You *could talk* to your teacher.	You *could have talked* to your teacher.
	(4) less than 50% certainty	--Where's John? He *could be* at home.	He *could have been* at home.
	(5) impossibility (*negative only*)	That *couldn't be* true!	That *couldn't have been* true!
be able to	(1) ability	I *am able to help* you. I *will be able to help* you.	I *was able to help* him.
would	(1) polite request	*Would* you please *pass* the salt? *Would* you *mind* if I left early?	
	(2) preference	I *would rather go* to the park than *stay* home.	I *would rather have gone* to the park.
	(3) repeated action in the past		When I was a child, I *would visit* my grandparents every weekend.
used to	(1) repeated action in the past		I *used to* visit my grandparents every weekend.
shall	(1) polite question to make a suggestion	*Shall* I *open* the window?	
	(2) future with "I" or "we" as subject	I *shall* arrive at nine. (*will = more common*)	

Note: Use of modals in reported speech is discussed in Chapter 7. Use of modals in conditional sentences is discussed in Chapter 10.

CHAPTER *3*

The Passive

3–1 FORMING THE PASSIVE

ACTIVE: (a) Mary **helped** the boy.	Form of the passive: **be** + *past participle*.
PASSIVE: (b) The boy **was helped** by Mary.	In the passive, *the object* of an active verb *becomes the subject* of the passive verb: "the boy" in (a) becomes the subject of the passive verb in (b). (a) and (b) have the same meaning.
ACTIVE: (c) An accident **happened**. PASSIVE: (d) *(none)*	Only transitive verbs (verbs that are followed by an object) are used in the passive. It is not possible to use verbs such as **happen**, **sleep**, **come**, and **seem** (intransitive verbs) in the passive. (See Appendix 1, Chart A-1.)

For the active sentence (a), the subject and verb are marked: S V O above "Mary helped the boy." For the passive sentence (b), S V is marked above "The boy was helped."

	ACTIVE			**PASSIVE**	
simple present	Mary	**helps**	John.	John	**is helped**	by Mary.
present progressive	Mary	**is helping**	John.	John	**is being helped**	by Mary.
present perfect	Mary	**has helped**	John.	John	**has been helped**	by Mary.
simple past	Mary	**helped**	John.	John	**was helped**	by Mary.
past progressive	Mary	**was helping**	John.	John	**was being helped**	by Mary.
past perfect	Mary	**had helped**	John.	John	**had been helped**	by Mary.
simple future	Mary	**will help**	John.	John	**will be helped**	by Mary.
be going to	Mary	**is going to help**	John.	John	**is going to be helped**	by Mary.
future perfect*	Mary	**will have helped**	John.	John	**will have been helped**	by Mary.

*The progressive forms of the present perfect, past perfect, future, and future perfect are very rarely used in the passive.

The wagon **is being pulled** by two horses.

3-2 USING THE PASSIVE

(a) Rice *is grown* in India. (b) Our house *was built* in 1890. (c) This olive oil *was imported* from Spain.	Usually the passive is used without a "*by* phrase." The passive is most frequently used when it is not known or not important to know exactly who performs an action. In (a): Rice is grown in India by people, by farmers, by someone. In sentence (a), it is not known or important to know exactly who grows rice in India. (a), (b), and (c) illustrate the most common use of the passive, i.e., without the "*by* phrase."
(d) *Life on the Mississippi was written* by Mark Twain.	The "*by* phrase" is included only if it is important to know who performs an action. In (d), *by Mark Twain* is important information.
(e) My aunt *made* this rug. (*active*) (f) This rug *was made* by my aunt. That rug *was made* by my mother.	If the speaker/writer knows who performs an action, usually the active is used, as in (e).
	The passive may be used with the "*by* phrase" instead of the active when the speaker/writer wants to focus attention on the subject of a sentence. In (f) the focus of attention is on two rugs.

3-3 INDIRECT OBJECTS AS PASSIVE SUBJECTS

I.O. **D.O.** (a) Someone gave **Mrs. Lee** an award. (b) **Mrs. Lee** was given an award.	**I.O.** = indirect object. **D.O.** = direct object. Either an indirect object or a direct object may become the subject of a passive sentence.
(c) Someone gave *an award* to Mrs. Lee. (d) *An award* was given to Mrs. Lee.	(a), (b), (c), and (d) have the same meaning. Note in (d): When the direct object becomes the subject, *to* is usually used in front of the indirect object.★

★The omission of *to* is more common in British English than American English: *An award was given Mrs. Lee.*

3–4 THE PASSIVE FORM OF MODALS AND SIMILAR EXPRESSIONS*

		THE PASSIVE FORM: *modal + **be** + past participle*	
(a) Tom	*will*	*be invited*	to the picnic.
(b) The window	*can't*	*be opened*.	
(c) Children	*should*	*be taught*	to respect their elders.
(d)	*May I*	*be excused*	from class?
(e) This book	*had better*	*be returned*	to the library before Friday.
(f) This letter	*ought to*	*be sent*	before June 1st.
(g) Mary	*has to*	*be told*	about our change in plans.
(h) Fred	*is supposed to*	*be told*	about the meeting.
		THE PAST-PASSIVE FORM: *modal + **have been** + past participle*	
(i) The letter	*should*	*have been sent*	last week.
(j) This house	*must*	*have been built*	over 200 years ago.
(k) Jack	*ought to*	*have been invited*	to the party.

*See Chapter 2 for a discussion of the form, meaning, and use of modals and similar expressions.

Does the pilot see an Unidentified Flying Object?
Some UFO sightings *cannot be explained* easily.

3-5 STATIVE PASSIVE

(a) The door *is old*. (b) The door *is green*. (c) The door *is locked*.	In (a) and (b): *old* and *green* are adjectives. They describe the door. In (c): *locked* is a past participle. It is used as an adjective. It describes the door.
(d) I locked the door five minutes ago. (e) The door was locked by me five minutes ago. (f) Now the door *is locked*.	The passive form may be used to describe an existing situation or state, as in (f) and (i). No action is taking place. The action happened before. There is no "*by* phrase." The past participle functions as an adjective.
(g) Ann broke the window. (h) The window was broken by Ann. (i) Now the window *is broken*.	When the passive form expresses an existing state rather than an action, it is called the "stative passive."
(j) I **am interested** *in* Chinese art. (k) He **is satisfied** *with* his job. (l) Ann **is married** *to* Alex.	Often stative passive verbs are followed by a preposition other than *by*. (See Appendix 2.)
(m) I don't know where I am. I **am lost**. (n) I can't find my purse. It **is gone**. (o) I **am finished with** my work. (p) I **am done with** my work.	(m) through (p) are examples of idiomatic usage of the passive form. These sentences have no equivalent active sentences.

Sam can't open the window.
It **is stuck**.

3–6 THE PASSIVE WITH *GET*

(a) I'm **getting hungry**. Let's eat soon. (b) You shouldn't eat so much. You'**ll get fat**. (c) I stopped working because I **got sleepy**.	**Get** may be followed by certain adjectives.*
(d) I stopped working because I **got tired**. (e) They **are getting married** next month. (f) I **got worried** because he was two hours late.	**Get** may also be followed by a past participle. The past participle functions as an adjective; it describes the subject. The passive with **get** is common in spoken English but is often not appropriate in formal writing.

*Some of the common adjectives that follow **get** are: *angry, anxious, bald, better, big, busy, chilly, cold, dark, dizzy, empty, fat, full, good, heavy, hot, hungry, late, light, mad, nervous, old, rich, sick, sleepy, tall, thirsty, warm, well, wet, worse.*

3–7 PARTICIPIAL ADJECTIVES

--The problem confuses the students. (a) It is a **confusing** problem.	The present participle conveys an active meaning. The noun it modifies does something. In (a): The noun "problem" does something; it "confuses." Thus, it is described as a "confusing problem."
--The students are confused by the problem. (b) They are **confused** students.	The past participle conveys a passive meaning. In (b): The students are confused by something. Thus, they are described as "confused students."
--The story amuses the children. (c) It is an **amusing** story.	In (c): The noun "story" performs the action.
--The children are amused by the story. (d) They are **amused** children.	In (d): The noun "children" receives the action.

There is an old saying: Let **sleeping** dogs lie.

CHAPTER *4*
Gerunds and Infinitives

A gerund = *the -ing form of a verb* (e.g., talking, playing, understanding).

An infinitive = *to + the simple form of a verb* (e.g., to talk, to play, to understand).

4–1 GERUNDS: INTRODUCTION

<table>
<tr>
<td>

    S   **V**
(a) ***Playing*** tennis is fun.

     S   **V**   **O**
(b) We enjoy ***playing*** tennis.

             PREP   **O**
(c) He's excited about ***playing*** tennis.

</td>
<td>

A gerund is the ***-ing*** form of a verb used as a noun.* A gerund is used in the same ways as a noun, i.e., as a subject or an object.

In (a): ***playing*** is a gerund. It is used as the subject of the sentence. ***Playing tennis*** is a gerund phrase.

In (b): ***playing*** is used as the object of the verb *enjoy.*

In (c): ***playing*** is used as the object of the preposition *about.*

</td>
</tr>
</table>

*COMPARE the uses of the ***-ing*** form of verbs:
    (1) ***Walking*** is good exercise. → ***walking*** = a gerund, used as the subject of the sentence.
    (2) Bob and Ann are ***playing*** tennis. → ***playing*** = a present participle, used in the present progressive tense.
    (3) I heard some ***surprising*** news. → ***surprising*** = a present participle, used as an adjective.

It is fun ***to sleep*** in a tent.
    (*infinitive*)

Sleeping in a tent is fun.
(*gerund*)

4–2 USING GERUNDS AS THE OBJECTS OF PREPOSITIONS

(a) We talked **about going** to Canada for our vacation. (b) Sue is in charge **of organizing** the meeting. (c) I'm interested **in learning** more about your work.	A gerund is frequently used as the object of a preposition.
(d) I**'m used to sleeping** with the window open. (e) I**'m accustomed to sleeping*** with the window open. (f) I **look forward to going** home next month. (g) They **object to changing** their plans at this late date.	In (d) through (g): **to** is a preposition, not part of an infinitive form, so a gerund follows.
(h) We **talked about not going** to the meeting, but finally decided we should go.	Negative form: **not** precedes a gerund.

*Possible in British English: *I'm accustomed to sleep with the window open.*

One day when Sally and Timmy were kids, they talked **about doing** something that they had never done before.

"Let's explore a cave," said Sally.

"I don't know where any caves are," replied Timmy. "I have a better idea. Let's smoke Uncle Ben's cigars!"

So they sneaked a couple of cigars out of their uncle's house. They were scared **of getting** caught by their parents, so they went down the street to a vacant lot. Neither of them was used **to smoking**. Sally complained **about feeling** sick to her stomach, and Timmy got very dizzy. They hated the cigars and never smoked again in their lives.

To this day, neither one of them approves **of smoking**.

4–3 COMMON VERBS FOLLOWED BY GERUNDS

VERB + GERUND (a) I *enjoy playing* tennis.	Gerunds are used as the objects of certain verbs. In (a), *enjoy* is followed by a gerund (*playing*). *Enjoy* is not followed by an infinitive. *INCORRECT: I enjoy to play tennis.* Common verbs that are followed by gerunds are given in the list below.
(b) Joe *quit smoking*. (c) Joe *gave up smoking*.	(b) and (c) have the same meaning. Some two-word verbs, e.g., *give up*, are followed by gerunds. These two-word verbs are given in parentheses in the list below.

VERB + GERUND

enjoy	*quit (give up)*	*avoid*	*consider (think about)*
appreciate	*finish (get through)*	*postpone (put off)*	*discuss (talk about)*
mind	*stop★*	*delay*	*mention*
		keep (keep on)	*suggest*

★*Stop* can also be followed immediately by an infinitive of purpose (*in order to*). See Chart 4-11.
  COMPARE the following:
  (1) *stop* + *gerund*: When the professor entered the room, the students *stopped talking*. The room became quiet.
  (2) *stop* + *infinitive of purpose*: While I was walking down the street, I ran into an old friend. I *stopped to talk* to him. (I stopped walking *in order to talk* to him.)

Ivan *enjoys* **hiking**.

He *goes* **hiking** every weekend during summer.

4–4   *GO* + GERUND

(a) Did you *go shopping*? (b) We *went fishing* yesterday.	*Go* is followed by a gerund in certain idiomatic expressions to express, for the most part, recreational activities.

GO + GERUND

go birdwatching	*go hiking*	*go sightseeing*
go boating	*go hunting*	*go skating*
go bowling	*go jogging*	*go skiing*
go camping	*go mountain climbing*	*go sledding*
go canoeing	*go running*	*go swimming*
go dancing	*go sailing*	*go tobogganing*
go fishing	*go shopping*	*go window shopping*

4–5 COMMON VERBS FOLLOWED BY INFINITIVES

VERB + INFINITIVE (a) I *hope to see* you again soon. (b) He *promised to be* here by ten. (c) He *promised not to be* late.	Some verbs are followed immediately by an infinitive, as in (a) and (b). See Group A below. Negative form: *not* precedes the infinitive.
VERB + (PRO)NOUN + INFINITIVE (d) Mr. Lee *told me to be* here at ten o'clock. (e) The police *ordered the driver to stop*.	Some verbs are followed by a (pro)noun and then an infinitive, as in (d) and (e). See Group B below.
(f) I *was told to be* here at ten o'clock. (g) The driver *was ordered to stop*.	These verbs are followed immediately by an infinitive when they are used in the passive, as in (f) and (g).
(h) I *expect to pass* the test. (i) I *expect Mary to pass* the test.	*Ask, expect, would like, want,* and *need* may or may not be followed by a (pro)noun object. COMPARE: In (h): I think I will pass the test. In (i): I think Mary will pass the test.

GROUP A: VERB + INFINITIVE

hope to	*promise* to	*seem* to	*ask* to
plan to	*agree* to	*appear* to	*expect* to
intend to★	*offer* to	*pretend* to	*would like* to
decide to	*refuse* to		*want* to
			need to

GROUP B: VERB + (PRO)NOUN + INFINITIVE

tell someone to	*invite* someone to	*require* someone to	*ask* someone to
advise someone to★★	*permit* someone to	*order* someone to	*expect* someone to
encourage someone to	*allow* someone to	*force* someone to	*would like* someone to
remind someone to	*warn* someone to		*want* someone to
			need someone to

★*Intend* is usually followed by an infinitive (*I intend to go* to the meeting) but sometimes may be followed by a gerund (*I intend going* to the meeting) with no change in meaning.
★★A gerund is used after *advise* (active) if there is no (pro)noun object. COMPARE:
    (1) He *advised buying* a Fiat.
    (2) He *advised me to buy* a Fiat. I *was advised to buy* a Fiat.

4-6 COMMON VERBS FOLLOWED BY EITHER INFINITIVES OR GERUNDS

Some verbs can be followed by either an infinitive or a gerund, sometimes with no difference in meaning, as in Group A below, and sometimes with a difference in meaning, as in Group B below.

GROUP A: VERB + INFINITIVE OR GERUND (WITH NO DIFFERENCE IN MEANING)

begin	*like*	*hate*	The verbs in Group A may be followed by either an infinitive or a gerund with little or no difference in meaning.
start	*love*	*can't stand*	
continue	*prefer*★	*can't bear*	

(a) It **began to rain**. / It **began raining**.	In (a): There is no difference between "began to rain" and "began raining."
(b) I **started to work**. / I **started working**.	
(c) It **was beginning to rain**.	If the main verb is progressive, an infinitive (not a gerund) is usually used.

GROUP B: VERB + INFINITIVE OR GERUND (WITH A DIFFERENCE IN MEANING)

| *remember* | *regret* | The verbs in Group B may be followed by either an infinitive or a gerund, but the meaning is different. |
| *forget* | *try* | |

(d) Judy always **remembers to lock** the door.	**Remember** + *infinitive* = remember to perform responsibility, duty, or task, as in (d).
(e) Sam often **forgets to lock** the door.	**Forget** + *infinitive* = forget to perform a responsibility, duty, or task, as in (e).
(f) I **remember seeing** the Alps for the first time. The sight was impressive.	**Remember** + *gerund* = remember (recall) something that happened in the past, as in (f).
(g) I'**ll never forget seeing** the Alps for the first time.	**Forget** + *gerund* = forget something that happened in the past, as in (g).★★
(h) I **regret to tell** you that you failed the test.	**Regret** + *infinitive* = regret to say, to tell someone, to inform someone of some bad news, as in (h).
(i) I **regret lending** him some money. He never paid me back.	**Regret** + *gerund* = regret something that happened in the past, as in (i).
(j) I'**m trying to learn** English.	**Try** + *infinitive* = make an effort, as in (j).
(k) The room was hot. I **tried opening** the window, but that didn't help. So I **tried turning** on the fan, but I was still hot. Finally, I turned on the air conditioner.	**Try** + *gerund* = experiment with a new or different approach to see if it works, as in (k).

★Notice the patterns with **prefer**:
   prefer + *gerund:* I **prefer staying** home **to going** to the concert.
   prefer + *infinitive:* I **prefer to stay** home **than (to) go** to the concert.

★★**Forget** followed by a gerund usually occurs in a negative sentence or a question: e.g., *I'll never forget, I can't forget, Have you ever forgotten,* and *Can you ever forget* can be followed by a gerund phrase.

4–7 REFERENCE LIST OF VERBS FOLLOWED BY GERUNDS

1.	*admit*	He *admitted stealing* the money.
2.	*advise*	She *advised waiting* until tomorrow.
3.	*anticipate*	I *anticipate having* a good time on vacation.
4.	*appreciate*	I *appreciated hearing* from them.
5.	*avoid*	He *avoided answering* my question.
6.	*complete*	I finally *completed writing* my term paper.
7.	*consider*	I *will consider going* with you.
8.	*delay*	He *delayed leaving* for school.
9.	*deny*	She *denied committing* the crime.
10.	*discuss*	They *discussed opening* a new business.
11.	*dislike*	I *dislike driving* long distances.
12.	*enjoy*	We *enjoyed visiting* them.
13.	*finish*	She *finished studying* about ten.
14.	*forget*	I'*ll never forget visiting* Napoleon's tomb.
15.	*can't help*	I *can't help worrying* about it.
16.	*keep*	I *keep hoping* he will come.
17.	*mention*	She *mentioned going* to a movie.
18.	*mind*	*Would* you *mind helping* me with this?
19.	*miss*	I *miss being* with my family.
20.	*postpone*	Let's *postpone leaving* until tomorrow.
21.	*practice*	The athlete *practiced throwing* the ball.
22.	*quit*	He *quit trying* to solve the problem.
23.	*recall*	I *don't recall meeting* him before.
24.	*recollect*	I *don't recollect meeting* him before.
25.	*recommend*	She *recommended seeing* the show.
26.	*regret*	I *regret telling* him my secret.
27.	*remember*	I *can remember meeting* him when I was a child.
28.	*resent*	I *resent her interfering* in my business.
29.	*resist*	I *couldn't resist eating* the dessert.
30.	*risk*	She *risks losing* all of her money.
31.	*stop*	She *stopped going* to classes when she got sick.
32.	*suggest*	She *suggested going* to a movie.
33.	*tolerate*	She *won't tolerate cheating* during an examination.
34.	*understand*	I *don't understand his leaving* school.

4–8 REFERENCE LIST OF VERBS FOLLOWED BY INFINITIVES

A. VERBS FOLLOWED IMMEDIATELY BY AN INFINITIVE

1.	*afford*	I *can't afford to buy* it.
2.	*agree*	They *agreed to help* us.
3.	*appear*	She *appears to be* tired.
4.	*arrange*	I'll *arrange to meet* you at the airport.
5.	*ask*	He *asked to come* with us.
6.	*beg*	He *begged to come* with us.
7.	*care*	I *don't care to see* that show.
8.	*claim*	She *claims to know* a famous movie star.
9.	*consent*	She finally *consented to marry* him.

10.	*decide*	I *have decided to leave* on Monday.
11.	*demand*	I *demand to know* who is responsible.
12.	*deserve*	She *deserves to win* the prize.
13.	*expect*	I *expect to enter* graduate school in the fall.
14.	*fail*	She *failed to return* the book to the library on time.
15.	*forget*	I *forgot to mail* the letter.
16.	*hesitate*	*Don't hesitate to ask* for my help.
17.	*hope*	Jack *hopes to arrive* next week.
18.	*learn*	He *learned to play* the piano.
19.	*manage*	She *managed to finish* her work early.
20.	*mean*	I *didn't mean to hurt* your feelings.
21.	*need*	I *need to have* your opinion.
22.	*offer*	They *offered to help* us.
23.	*plan*	I *am planning to have* a party.
24.	*prepare*	We *prepared to welcome* them.
25.	*pretend*	He *pretends not to understand*.
26.	*promise*	I *promise not to be* late.
27.	*refuse*	I *refuse to believe* his story.
28.	*regret*	I *regret to tell* you that you failed.
29.	*remember*	I *remembered to lock* the door.
30.	*seem*	That cat *seems to be* friendly.
31.	*struggle*	I *struggled to stay* awake.
32.	*swear*	She *swore to tell* the truth.
33.	*threaten*	She *threatened to tell* my parents.
34.	*volunteer*	He *volunteered to help* us.
35.	*wait*	I *will wait to hear* from you.
36.	*want*	I *want to tell* you something.
37.	*wish*	She *wishes to come* with us.

B. VERBS FOLLOWED BY A (PRO)NOUN + AN INFINITIVE

38.	*advise*	She *advised me to wait* until tomorrow.
39.	*allow*	She *allowed me to use* her car.
40.	*ask*	I *asked John to help* us.
41.	*beg*	They *begged us to come*.
42.	*cause*	Her laziness *caused her to fail*.
43.	*challenge*	She *challenged me to race* her to the corner.
44.	*convince*	I couldn't *convince him to accept* our help.
45.	*dare*	He *dared me to do* better than he had done.
46.	*encourage*	He *encouraged me to try* again.
47.	*expect*	I *expect you to be* on time.
48.	*forbid*	I *forbid you to tell* him.
49.	*force*	They *forced him to tell* the truth.
50.	*hire*	She *hired a boy to mow* the lawn.
51.	*instruct*	He *instructed them to be careful.*
52.	*invite*	Harry *invited the Johnsons to come* to his party.
53.	*need*	We *needed Chris to help* us figure out the solution.
54.	*order*	The judge *ordered me to pay* a fine.
55.	*permit*	He *permitted the children to stay* up late.
56.	*persuade*	I *persuaded him to come* for a visit.
57.	*remind*	She *reminded me to lock* the door.
58.	*require*	Our teacher *requires us to be* on time.
59.	*teach*	My brother *taught me to swim*.
60.	*tell*	The doctor *told me to take* these pills.
61.	*urge*	I *urged her to apply* for the job.
62.	*want*	I *want you to be* happy.
63.	*warn*	I *warned you not to drive* too fast.

4–9 USING GERUNDS AS SUBJECTS; USING *IT* + INFINITIVE

(a) **Riding** *with a drunk driver* is dangerous.	A gerund is frequently used as the subject of a sentence, as in (a).
(b) **To ride** *with a drunk driver* is dangerous. (c) **It** is dangerous **to ride** *with a drunk driver*.	Sometimes an infinitive is used as the subject of a sentence, as in (b). However, an infinitive is more commonly used with **it**, as in (c). The word **it** refers to and has the same meaning as the infinitive phrase at the end of the sentence.*

*Sometimes a gerund is used with **it** when the speaker is talking about a particular situation and wants to give the idea of "while": *Tom was drunk. It was dangerous* **riding** *with him.* = *We were in danger while we were riding with him.*

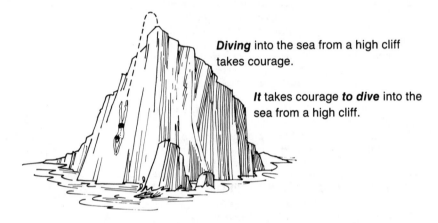

Diving into the sea from a high cliff takes courage.

It takes courage **to dive** into the sea from a high cliff.

4–10 INFINITIVE OF PURPOSE: *IN ORDER TO*

(a) He came here **in order to study** English. (b) He came here **to study** English.	**In order to** is used to express *purpose*. It answers the question "Why?" **In order** is often omitted, as in (b).
(c) *INCORRECT: He came here for studying English.* (d) *INCORRECT: He came here for to study English.* (e) *INCORRECT: He came here for study English.*	To express purpose, use (**in order**) **to** not **for**, with a verb.*
(f) I went to the store **for** some bread. (g) I went to the store **to buy** some bread.	**For** is sometimes used to express purpose, but it is a preposition and is followed by a noun object, as in (f).

*Exception: The phrase **be used for** expresses the typical or general purpose of a thing. In this case, the preposition **for** is followed by a gerund: *A saw* **is used for cutting** *wood.* Also possible: *A saw* **is used to cut** *wood.*
However, to talk about a particular thing and a particular situation, **be used** + *an infinitive* is used: *A chain saw* **was used to cut** *down the old oak tree.* (*INCORRECT: A chain saw was used for cutting down the old oak tree.*)

4-11   ADJECTIVES FOLLOWED BY INFINITIVES

(a) We **were sorry to hear** the bad news. (b) I **was surprised to see** Tim at the meeting.	Certain adjectives can be immediately followed by infinitives, as in (a) and (b). In general, these adjectives describe a person (or persons), not a thing. Many of these adjectives describe a person's feelings or attitudes.

SOME COMMON ADJECTIVES FOLLOWED BY INFINITIVES

glad to	*sorry to*★	*ready to*	*careful to*	*surprised to*★
happy to	*sad to*★	*prepared to*	*hesitant to*	*amazed to*★
pleased to	*upset to*★	*anxious to*	*reluctant to*	*astonished to*★
delighted to	*disappointed to*★	*eager to*	*afraid to*	*shocked to*★
content to		*willing to*		*stunned to*★
relieved to	*proud to*	*motivated to*		
lucky to	*ashamed to*	*determined to*		
fortunate to				

*The expressions with asterisks are usually followed by infinitive phrases with verbs such as **see, learn, discover, find out, hear**.

4-12   USING INFINITIVES WITH *TOO* AND *ENOUGH*

(a) That box is **too heavy** for Bob **to lift**. COMPARE: (b) That box is **very heavy**, but Bob can lift it.	In the speaker's mind, the use of **too** implies a negative result. In (a): **too heavy** = It is *impossible* for Bob to lift that box. In (b): **very heavy** = It is *possible but difficult* for Bob to lift that box.
(c) I am **strong enough** *to lift* that box. I can lift it.	**Enough** follows an adjective, as in (c).
(d) I have **enough strength** *to lift* that box. (e) I have **strength enough** *to lift* that box.	**Enough** may precede a noun, as in (d), or follow a noun, as in (e).

4–13 PASSIVE AND PAST FORMS OF INFINITIVES AND GERUNDS

PASSIVE INFINITIVE: **to be** + *past participle* (a) I didn't expect **to be invited** to his party.	In (a): **to be invited** is passive. The understood "**by** phrase" is "by him": *I didn't expect to be invited by him.*
PASSIVE GERUND: **being** + *past participle* (b) I appreciated **being invited** to your home.	In (b): **being invited** is passive. The understood "**by** phrase" is "by you": *I appreciated being invited by you.*
PAST INFINITIVE: **to have** + *past participle* (c) The rain seems **to have stopped**.	The event expressed by a past infinitive or past gerund happened before the time of the main verb. In (c): *The rain seems now to have stopped a few minutes ago.* ★
PAST GERUND: **having** + *past participle* (d) I appreciate **having had** the opportunity to meet the king.	In (d): I met the king yesterday. *I appreciate now having had the opportunity to meet the king yesterday.* ★
PAST-PASSIVE INFINITIVE: 　　**to have been** + *past participle* (e) Jane is fortunate **to have been given** a scholarship.	In (e): Jane was given a scholarship last month by her government. She is fortunate. *Jane is fortunate now to have been given a scholarship last month by her government.*
PAST-PASSIVE GERUND: 　　**having been** + *past participle* (f) I appreciate **having been told** the news.	In (f): I was told the news yesterday by someone. I appreciate that. *I appreciate now having been told the news yesterday by someone.*

★If the main verb is past, the action of the past infinitive or gerund happened before a time in the past:
　　*The rain **seemed to have stopped**.* = The rain seemed at six P.M. to have stopped before six P.M.
　　*I **appreciated having had** the opportunity to meet the king.* = I met the king in 1985. I appreciated in 1987 having had the opportunity to meet the king in 1985.

Susan doesn't like **being forced** to leave the room *(in order) to study* whenever her roommate feels like *having* a party.

4-14 USING GERUNDS OR PASSIVE INFINITIVES FOLLOWING *NEED*

(a) I **need to borrow** some money. (b) John **needs to be told** the truth.	Usually an infinitive follows **need**, as in (a) and (b).
(c) The house **needs painting**. (d) The house **needs to be painted**.	In certain situations, a gerund may follow **need**. In this case, the gerund carries a passive meaning. Usually the situations involve fixing or improving something. (c) and (d) have the same meaning.

4-15 USING A POSSESSIVE TO MODIFY A GERUND

We came to class late. Mr. Lee complained about that fact. (a) FORMAL: Mr. Lee complained about **our coming** to class late.*	In formal English, a possessive pronoun (e.g., **our**) is used to modify a gerund, as in (a).
(b) INFORMAL: Mr. Lee complained about **us coming** to class late.	In informal English, the object form (e.g., **us**) is frequently used, as in (b).
(c) FORMAL: Mr. Lee complained about **Mary's coming** to class late.	In very formal English, a possessive noun (e.g., **Mary's**) is used to modify a gerund.
(d) INFORMAL: Mr. Lee complained about **Mary coming** to class late.	The possessive form is often not used in informal English, as in (d).

*"Coming to class late" occurred before "Mr. Lee complained," so a past gerund is also possible: *Mr. Lee complained about **our having come** to class late.*

4–16 USING VERBS OF PERCEPTION

(a) I **saw** my friend **run** down the street. (b) I **saw** my friend **running** down the street. (c) I **heard** the rain **fall** on the roof. (d) I **heard** the rain **falling** on the roof.	Certain verbs of perception are followed by either *the simple form** or *the **-ing** form*** of a verb. There is usually little difference in meaning between the two forms except that the **-ing** form usually gives the idea of "while." In (b): I saw my friend while she was running down the street.
(e) I **heard** a famous opera star **sing** at the concert last night. (f) When I walked into the apartment, I **heard** my roommate **singing** in the shower.	Sometimes (not always) there is a clear difference between using the simple form or the **-ing** form. In (e): I heard the singing from beginning to end. In (f): The singing was in progress when I heard it.

VERBS OF PERCEPTION FOLLOWED BY THE SIMPLE FORM OR THE *-ING* FORM			
see *notice* *watch* *look at* *observe*	*hear* *listen to*	*feel*	*smell*

*The simple form of a verb = the infinitive form without "to."
    INCORRECT: I saw my friend to run down the street.
The **-ing form refers to the present participle.

4–17 USING THE SIMPLE FORM AFTER *LET* AND *HELP*

(a) My father **let** me **drive** his car. (b) I **let** my friend **borrow** my bicycle.	**Let** is always followed by the simple form of a verb, not an infinitive. (*INCORRECT: My father let me to drive his car.*)
(c) My brother **helped** me **wash** my car. (d) My brother **helped** me **to wash** my car.	**Help** is often followed by the simple form of a verb, as in (c). An infinitive is also possible, as in (d). Both (c) and (d) are correct.

4–18 USING CAUSATIVE VERBS: *MAKE, HAVE, GET*

(a) I *made* my brother *carry* my suitcase. (b) I *had* my brother *carry* my suitcase. (c) I *got* my brother *to carry* my suitcase. FORM: X *makes* Y *do* something. (simple form) X *has* Y *do* something. (simple form) X *gets* Y *to do* something. (infinitive)	*Make, have,* and *get* can be used to express the idea that "X" causes "Y" to do something. When they are used as causative verbs, their meanings are similar but not identical. In (a): My brother had no choice. I insisted that he carry my suitcase. In (b): My brother carried my suitcase simply because I asked him to. In (c): I managed to persuade my brother to carry my suitcase.
(d) Mrs. Lee *made* her son *clean* his room. (e) Sad movies *make* me *cry*.	Causative *make* is followed by the simple form of a verb, not an infinitive. (*INCORRECT: She made him to clean his room.*) *Make* gives the idea that "X" forces "Y" to do something. In (d): Mrs. Lee's son had no choice.
(f) I *had* the plumber *repair* the leak. (g) Jane *had* the waiter *bring* her some tea.	Causative *have* is followed by the simple form of a verb, not an infinitive. (*INCORRECT: I had him to repair the leak.*) *Have* gives the idea that "X" requests "Y" to do something. In (f): The plumber repaired the leak because I asked him to.
(h) The students *got* the teacher *to dismiss* class early. (i) Jack *got* his friends *to play* soccer with him after school.	Causative *get* is followed by an infinitive. *Get* gives the idea that "X" persuades "Y" to do something. In (h): The students managed to persuade the teacher to let them leave early.
(j) I *had* my watch *repaired* (by someone). (k) I *got* my watch *repaired* (by someone).	The past participle is used after *have* and *get* to give a passive meaning. In this case, there is usually little or no difference in meaning between *have* and *get*. In (j) and (k): I caused my watch to be repaired by someone.

There's an old saying: You can lead a horse to water, but you can't *make* him *drink*.

4–19 SPECIAL EXPRESSIONS FOLLOWED BY THE -ING FORM OF A VERB

(a) We *had fun* We *had a good time* } *playing* volleyball.	*have fun* + *-ing* *have a good time* + *-ing*
(b) I *had trouble* I *had difficulty* I *had a hard time* I *had a difficult time* } *finding* his house.	*have trouble* + *-ing* *have difficulty* + *-ing* *have a hard time* + *-ing* *have a difficult time* + *-ing*
(c) Sam *spends* most of his time *studying*. (d) I *waste* a lot of time *watching* TV.	*spend* + *expression of time or money* + *-ing* *waste* + *expression of time or money* + *-ing*
(e) She *sat* at her desk *writing* a letter. (f) I *stood* there *wondering* what to do next. (g) He *is lying* in bed *reading* a novel.	*sit* + *expression of place* + *-ing* *stand* + *expression of place* + *-ing* *lie* + *expression of place* + *-ing*
(h) When I walked into my office, I *found* George *using* my telephone. (i) When I walked into my office, I *caught* a thief *looking* through my desk drawers.	*find* + *(pro)noun* + *-ing* *catch* + *(pro)noun* + *-ing* In (h) and (i): Both *find* and *catch* mean discover. *Catch* expresses anger or displeasure.

CHAPTER 5
Singular and Plural

5-1 FINAL -*S*/-*ES*

(a) NOUN + -*S*: *Friends* are important. NOUN + -*ES*: I like my *classes*.	A final -*s* or -*es* is added to a noun to make a noun plural. *friend* = *a singular noun* *friends* = *a plural noun*

(b) VERB + -*S*:   John *works* at the bank.
VERB + -*ES*: She *watches* birds.
	A final -*s* or -*es* is added to a simple present verb when the subject is a singular noun or third person singular pronoun.*
	    John works = *singular* **The students work** = *plural*
	    He works = *singular* **They work** = *plural*

SPELLING: FINAL -*S* vs. -*ES* (c) sing → *sings* song → *songs*	For most words (whether a verb or a noun), simply a final -*s* is added to spell the word correctly.

(d) wash → *washes*
    watch → *watches*
    class → *classes*
    buzz → *buzzes*
    box   → *boxes*
	Final -*es* is added to words that end in -*sh*, -*ch*, -*s*, -*z*, and -*x*.

(e) toy   → *toys*
    buy   → *buys*
(f) baby → *babies*
    cry   → *cries*
	For words that end in -*y*:
	In (e): If -*y* is preceded by a vowel, only -*s* is added.
	In (f): If -*y* is preceded by a consonant, the -*y* is changed to -*i* and -*es* is added.

*A singular noun = *Mary, my father, the machine*.
 A third person singular subject pronoun = *she, he, it*.

A baby *cries*.
All *babies* cry.

5–2 IRREGULAR PLURAL NOUNS

The nouns in (a) have irregular plural forms:

(a) *man–men*   *child–children*   *mouse–mice*   *foot–feet*
    woman–women   *ox–oxen*   *louse–lice*   *goose–geese*
                                                                     tooth–teeth

Some nouns that end in *-o* add *-es* to form the plural:

(b) *echoes*   *heroes*   *potatoes*   *tomatoes*

Some nouns that end in *-o* add only *-s* to form the plural:

(c) *autos*   *photos*   *solos*   *tatoos*
    kilos   *pianos*   *sopranos*   *videos*
    memos   *radios*   *studios*   *zoos*

Some nouns that end in *-o* add either *-es* or *-s* to form the plural:

(d) *mosquitoes/mosquitos*   *volcanoes/volcanos*
    tornadoes/tornados   *zeroes/zeros*

Some nouns that end in *-f* or *-fe* are changed to *-ves* in the plural:

(e) *calf–calves*   *leaf–leaves*   *self–selves*   *wolf–wolves*
    half–halves   *life–lives*   *shelf–shelves*   *scarf–scarves/scarfs*
    knife–knives   *loaf–loaves*   *thief–thieves*

Some nouns that end in *-f* simply add *-s* to form the plural:

(f) *belief–beliefs*   *chief–chiefs*   *cliff–cliffs*   *roof–roofs*

Some nouns have the same singular and plural form: (e.g., One deer is . . . . Two deer are . . . .)

(g) *deer*   *fish*   *means*   *series*   *sheep*   *species*

Some nouns that English has borrowed from other languages have foreign plurals:

(h) *criterion–criteria*   (k) *analysis–analyses*   (m) *bacterium–bacteria*
    phenomenon–phenomena   *basis–bases*   *curriculum–curricula*
                                    crisis–crises   *datum–data*
(i) *cactus–cacti/cactuses*   *hypothesis–hypotheses*   *medium–media*
    stimulus–stimuli   *oasis–oases*   *memorandum–memoranda*
    syllabus–syllabi/syllabuses   *parenthesis–parentheses*
                                    thesis–theses

(j) *formula–formulae/formulas* (l) *appendix–appendices/appendixes*
    vertebra–vertebrae   *index–indices/indexes*

5-3 POSSESSIVE NOUNS

<table>
<tr><td colspan="2">(a) SINGULAR NOUN   POSSESSIVE FORM</td><td>To show possession, add an apostrophe (') and -s to a singular noun: The girl's book is on the table.</td></tr>
<tr><td>the girl
Tom</td><td>the girl's
Tom's</td><td rowspan="3">If a singular noun ends in -s, there are two possible forms:
    (1) Add an apostrophe and -s: Thomas's book.
    (2) Add only an apostrophe: Thomas' book.</td></tr>
<tr><td>my wife
a lady</td><td>my wife's
a lady's</td></tr>
<tr><td>Thomas</td><td>Thomas's/Thomas'</td></tr>
<tr><td colspan="2">(b) PLURAL NOUN   POSSESSIVE FORM</td><td>Add only an apostrophe to a plural noun that ends in -s: The girls' books are on the table.</td></tr>
<tr><td>the girls
their wives
the ladies</td><td>the girls'
their wives'
the ladies'</td><td rowspan="2">Add an apostrophe and -s to plural nouns that do not end in -s: The men's books are on the table.</td></tr>
<tr><td>the men
my children</td><td>the men's
my children's</td></tr>
</table>

There's a ball in the **boy's** pocket.

5-4 USING NOUNS AS MODIFIERS

<table>
<tr><td>(a) The soup has vegetables in it.
It is vegetable soup.
(b) The building has offices in it.
It is an office building.</td><td>Notice: When a noun is used as a modifier, it is in its singular form.</td></tr>
<tr><td>(c) The test lasted two hours.
It was a two-hour test.
(d) Her son is five years old.
She has a five-year-old son.</td><td>When a noun used as a modifier is combined with a number expression, the noun is singular and a hyphen (-) is used.</td></tr>
</table>

5-5 COUNT AND NONCOUNT NOUNS

(a) I bought *a chair*. Sam bought *three chairs*.	*Chair* is a count noun; chairs are items that can be counted.
(b) We bought *some furniture*. INCORRECT: *We bought a furniture.* INCORRECT: *We bought some furnitures.*	*Furniture* is a noncount noun. In grammar, furniture cannot be counted.

	SINGULAR	PLURAL	
COUNT NOUN	a chair one chair	chairs two chairs some chairs a lot of chairs many chairs★	A count noun: (1) may be preceded by *a/an* in the singular; (2) takes a final *-s/-es* in the plural.
NONCOUNT NOUN	furniture some furniture a lot of furniture much furniture★		A noncount noun: (1) is not immediately preceded by *a/an*; (2) has no plural form; does not take a final *-s/-es*.

★See Chart 5-8 for other expressions of quantity that are used with count and noncount nouns.

5-6 NONCOUNT NOUNS

Notice in the following: Most noncount nouns refer to a "whole" that is made up of different parts.	
(a) I bought some chairs, tables, and desks. In other words, I bought some *furniture*.	In (a): *furniture* represents a whole group of things that is made up of similar but separate items.
(b) I put some *sugar* in my *coffee*.	In (b): *sugar* and *coffee* represent whole masses made up of individual particles or elements.★
(c) I wish you *luck*.	In (c): *luck* is an abstract concept, an abstract "whole." It has no physical form; you can't touch it. You can't count it.
(d) *Sunshine* is warm and cheerful.	In (d): Phenomena of nature, such as *sunshine*, are frequently used as noncount nouns.
(e) NONCOUNT: Ann has brown *hair*. COUNT: Tom has *a hair* on his jacket.	Many nouns can be used as either noncount or count nouns, but the meaning is different; e.g., *hair* in (e) and *light* in (f).
(f) NONCOUNT: I opened the curtains to let in some *light*. COUNT: Don't forget to turn off the *lights* before you go to bed.	(Dictionaries written especially for learners of English as a second language are a good source of information on count/noncount usages of nouns.)

★To express a particular quantity, some noncount nouns may be preceded by unit expressions: e.g., *a spoonful of sugar, a glass of water, a cup of coffee, a quart of milk, a loaf of bread, a grain of rice, a bowl of soup, a bag of flour, a pound of meat, a piece of furniture, a piece of paper, a piece of jewelry.*

5-7 SOME COMMON NONCOUNT NOUNS

The following are typical of nouns that are commonly used as noncount nouns. Many other nouns can be used as noncount nouns. This list serves only as a sample.

(a) WHOLE GROUPS MADE UP OF SIMILAR ITEMS: *baggage, clothing, equipment, food, fruit, furniture, garbage, hardware, jewelry, junk, luggage, machinery, mail, makeup, money/cash/change, postage, scenery, traffic*

(b) FLUIDS: *water, coffee, tea, milk, oil, soup, gasoline, blood, etc.*
(c) SOLIDS: *ice, bread, butter, cheese, meat, gold, iron, silver, glass, paper, wood, cotton, wool, etc.*
(d) GASES: *steam, air, oxygen, nitrogen, smoke, smog, pollution, etc.*
(e) PARTICLES: *rice, chalk, corn, dirt, dust, flour, grass, hair, pepper, salt, sand, sugar, wheat, etc.*

(f) ABSTRACTIONS:
—*beauty, confidence, courage, education, enjoyment, fun, happiness, health, help, honesty, hospitality, importance, intelligence, justice, knowledge, laughter, luck, music, patience, peace, pride, progress, recreation, significance, sleep, truth, violence, wealth, etc.*
—*advice, information, news, evidence, proof*
—*time, space, energy*
—*homework, work*
—*grammar, slang, vocabulary*

(g) LANGUAGES: *Arabic, Chinese, English, Spanish, etc.*
(h) FIELDS OF STUDY: *chemistry, engineering, history, literature, mathematics, psychology, etc.*
(i) RECREATION: *baseball, soccer, tennis, chess, bridge, poker, etc.*
(j) GENERAL ACTIVITIES: *driving, studying, swimming, traveling, walking (and other gerunds)*

(k) NATURAL PHENOMENA: *weather, dew, fog, hail, heat, humidity, lightning, rain, sleet, snow, thunder, wind, darkness, light, sunshine, electricity, fire, gravity*

There are more stars in the universe than there are grains of **sand** on all the beaches on earth.

5–8 EXPRESSIONS OF QUANTITY

An expression of quantity (e.g., *one*, *several*, *many*, *much*) may precede a noun. *Notice below*: Some expressions of quantity are used only with count nouns; some only with noncount nouns; some with both count and noncount nouns.

EXPRESSIONS OF QUANTITY	USED WITH COUNT NOUNS	USED WITH NONCOUNT NOUNS
one	*one apple*	Ø★
each	*each apple*	Ø
every	*every apple*	Ø
two	*two apples*	Ø
both	*both apples*	Ø
a couple of	*a couple of apples*	Ø
three, etc.	*three apples*	Ø
a few	*a few apples*	Ø
several	*several apples*	Ø
many	*many apples*	Ø
a number of	*a number of apples*	Ø
a little	Ø	*a little rice*
much	Ø	*much rice*
a great deal of	Ø	*a great deal of rice*
not any/no	*not any/no apples*	*not any/no rice*
some	*some apples*	*some rice*
a lot of	*a lot of apples*	*a lot of rice*
lots of	*lots of apples*	*lots of rice*
plenty of	*plenty of apples*	*plenty of rice*
most	*most apples*	*most rice*
all	*all apples*	*all rice*

★Ø = "not used." For example, you can say "*I ate one apple*" but NOT "*I ate one rice.*"

one apple

many apples / much fruit
a number of apples / a great deal of fruit
a lot of apples / a lot of fruit
plenty of apples / plenty of fruit
some apples / some fruit

three apples
several apples
a few apples / a little fruit
some apples / some fruit

5-9 USING A FEW AND FEW; A LITTLE AND LITTLE

a few *a little*	(a) She has been here only two weeks, but she has already made **a few friends**. *(Positive idea: She has made some friends.)* (b) I'm very pleased. I've been able to save **a little money** this month. *(Positive idea: I have saved some money instead of spending all of it.)*	**A few** and **a little**★ give a positive idea; they indicate that something exists, is present, as in (a) and (b).
few *little*	(c) I feel sorry for her. She has **(very) few friends**. *(Negative idea: She does not have many friends; she has almost no friends.)* (d) I have **(very) little money**. I don't even have enough money to buy food for dinner. *(Negative idea: I do not have much money; I have almost no money.)*	**Few** and **little** (without **a**) give a negative idea; they indicate that something is largely absent. **Very** (+ **few/little**) makes the negative idea stronger, the number/amount smaller.

★**A few** and **few** are used with plural count nouns. **A little** and **little** are used with noncount nouns.

a little chicken   a little chicken   a few chickens

a big chicken   a lot of chicken   a lot of chickens

5-10 USING *OF* IN EXPRESSIONS OF QUANTITY

MOST + **NONSPECIFIC NOUN** (a) **Most books** are interesting.	In (a): The speaker is not referring to specific books. The speaker is not referring to "those books" or "your books" or "the books written by Mark Twain." The noun "books" is nonspecific.
(b) *INCORRECT: Most of books are interesting.*	In (b): The word *of* is not added to an expression of quantity (e.g., **most**) if the noun it modifies is nonspecific.
MOST + **OF** + **SPECIFIC NOUN** (c) Most **of those** books are mine. (d) Most **of my** books are in English. (e) Most **of the** books on that table are mine.	A noun is specific when it is preceded by: —**this**, **that**, **these**, **those**, as in (c); OR —**my**, **John's**, **their** (any possessive) as in (d); OR —**the**, as in (e). When a noun is specific, *of* is used with an expression of quantity.*

EXPRESSIONS OF QUANTITY FOLLOWED BY *OF* + A SPECIFIC NOUN
all, most, some/any + **of** + specific plural *count* noun or *noncount* noun, as in (f)   **many, (a) few, several, both, two, one** + **of** + specific plural *count* noun, as in (g)   **much, (a) little** + **of** + specific *noncount* noun, as in (h)

(f) *count:* **Most of those chairs** are uncomfortable.   *noncount:* **Most of that furniture** is uncomfortable.
(g) *count:* **Many of those chairs** are uncomfortable.
(h) *noncount:* **Much of that furniture** is uncomfortable.

*NOTE: *of* is always a part of the following expressions of quantity, whether the noun is nonspecific or specific: **a lot of, lots of, a couple of, plenty of, a number of, a great deal of**.
    NONSPECIFIC: I've read *a lot of books*.   SPECIFIC: I've read *a lot of those books*.

5-10.1 USING *OF* WITH *ALL* AND *BOTH*

(a) CORRECT: **All of the students** in my class are here. (b) CORRECT: **All the students** in my class are here.	When a noun is specific (e.g., *the students*), using *of* after **all** is optional.
(c) CORRECT: **All students** must have an I.D. card. (d) *INCORRECT: All of students must have an I.D. card.*	When a noun is nonspecific, *of* does NOT follow **all**.
(e) I know **both (of) those men**.	Similarly, using *of* after **both** is optional when the noun is specific.

5–11 SINGULAR EXPRESSIONS OF QUANTITY: ONE, EACH, EVERY

(a) **One student** was late to class. (b) **Each student** has a schedule. (c) **Every student** has a schedule.	**One**, **each**, and **every** are followed immediately by *singular count nouns* (never plural nouns, never non-count nouns).
(d) **One of the students** was late to class. (e) **Each (one) of the students** has a schedule. (f) **Every one of the students** has a schedule.	**One of**, **each of**, and **every one of*** are followed by *specific plural count nouns* (never singular nouns, never noncount nouns).

*COMPARE:
> **Every one** (spelled as two words) is an expression of quantity; e.g., *I have read **every one** of those books.*
> **Everyone** (spelled as one word) is an indefinite pronoun; it has the same meaning as **everybody**; e.g.,
> **Everyone/Everybody** has a schedule.

NOTE: **Each** and **every** have essentially the same meaning.
> **Each** is used when the speaker is thinking of one person/thing at a time: *Each student has a schedule. = Mary has a schedule. John has a schedule. Hiroshi has a schedule. Carlos has a schedule. Sabrina has a schedule. (etc.)*
> **Every** is used when the speaker means "all." *Every student has a schedule. = All of the students have schedules.*

5–12 BASIC SUBJECT–VERB AGREEMENT

SINGULAR VERB	PLURAL VERB	
(a) My *friend* **lives** in Boston.	(b) My *friends* **live** in Boston.	verb + **-s/-es** = third person singular in the simple present tense noun + **-s/-es** = plural
(c) That *book* on political parties **is** interesting.	(d) The *ideas* in that book **are** interesting.	A prepositional phrase that comes between a subject and a verb does not affect the verb.
	(e) My *brother and sister* **live** in Boston.	Two (or more) subjects connected by **and** take a plural verb.
(f) *Every man, woman, and child* **needs** love. (g) *Each book and magazine* **is** listed in the card catalog.		EXCEPTION: **Every** and **each** are always followed immediately by singular nouns. In this case, even when there are two (or more) nouns connected by **and**, the verb is singular.
(h) *Growing* flowers **is** her hobby.		A gerund used as the subject of a sentence takes a singular verb.

5-13 SUBJECT–VERB AGREEMENT: USING EXPRESSIONS OF QUANTITY

SINGULAR VERB	PLURAL VERB	

(a) *Some of the book **is*** good.
(c) *A lot of the equipment **is*** new.
(e) *Two-thirds of the money **is*** mine.
	(b) *Some of the books **are*** good.
	(d) *A lot of my friends **are*** here.
	(f) *Two-thirds of the pennies **are*** mine.
		The verb is determined by the noun (or pronoun) that follows ***of*** in most expressions of quantity. Notice in (a) and (b):
		    some of + *singular noun* + *singular verb*
		    some of + *plural noun* + *plural verb*

(g) *One of my friends **is*** here.
(h) *Each of my friends **is*** here.
(i) *Every one of my friends **is*** here.
		EXCEPTIONS: ***One of, each of***, and ***every one of*** take singular verbs.
		    one of
		    each of + *plural noun* + *singular verb*
		    every one of

(j) *None of the boys **is*** here.	(k) *None of the boys **are*** here. *(informal)*	Subjects with ***none of*** are considered singular in very formal English, but plural verbs are often used in informal speech and writing.
(l) *The number of students* in the class ***is*** fifteen.	(m) *A number of students **were*** late for class.	COMPARE: In (l): ***The number*** is the subject. In (m): ***A number of*** is an expression of quantity meaning "a lot of." It is followed by a plural noun and a plural verb.

5-14 SUBJECT–VERB AGREEMENT: USING *THERE + BE*

SINGULAR VERB	PLURAL VERB	
(a) There ***is*** *a book* on the shelf.	(b) There ***are*** *some books* on the shelf.	The subject follows ***be*** when ***there*** is used.* In (a): The subject is *book*. In (b): The subject is *books*.

*In the structure ***there + be***, *there* is called an *expletive*.

There is a bag in the picture.
There are groceries in the bag.

5–15 SUBJECT–VERB AGREEMENT: SOME IRREGULARITIES

SINGULAR VERB

(a) *The news **is** interesting.* (b) *The United States **is** big.* (c) *The Philippines **consists** of more than 7,000 islands.* (d) *The United Nations **has** its headquarters in New York City.* (e) *Sears **is** a department store.* (f) *Mathematics **is** easy for her. Physics **is** easy for her, too.*	Sometimes a noun that ends in **-s** is singular. Notice the examples: If the noun is changed to a pronoun, the singular pronoun **it** is used (not the plural pronoun **they**) because the noun is singular. In (a): **news** = **it** (not **they**). In (b): **the United States** = **it** (not **they**). Note: Fields of study, as in (f), that end in **-ics** take singular verbs.
(g) *Eight hours of sleep **is** enough.* (h) *Ten dollars **is** too much to pay.* (i) *Five thousand miles **is** too far to travel.*	Expressions of *time, money,* and *distance* usually take a singular verb.

PLURAL VERB

(j) *Those people **are** from Canada.* (k) *The police **have** been called.*	**People***** and **police** do not end in **-s** but are plural nouns and take plural verbs.

SINGULAR VERB   PLURAL VERB

(l) *English **is** spoken in many countries.* (n) *Chinese **is** his native language.*	(m) *The English **drink** tea.* (o) *The Chinese **have** an interesting history.*	In (l): **English** = language. In (m): **the English** = people from England. Some nouns of nationality that end in **-sh, -ese,** and **-ch** can mean either language or people; e.g., *English, Spanish, Chinese, Japanese, Vietnamese, Portuguese, French.*
	(p) *The poor **have** many problems.* (q) *The rich **get** richer.*	A few adjectives can be preceded by **the** and used as a plural noun (without final **-s**) to refer to people who have this quality. Other examples: *the young, the old, the living, the dead, the blind, the deaf, the handicapped.*

The word **people has a final **-s** (*peoples*) only when it is used to refer to nations or ethnic groups: *All the peoples of the world desire peace.*

5-16 PERSONAL PRONOUNS: AGREEMENT WITH NOUNS

(a) **A student** walked into the room. **She** was looking for the teacher.	A singular pronoun is used to refer to a singular noun, as in (a) and (b).
(b) **A student** walked into the room. **He** was looking for the teacher.	
(c) **Some students** walked into the room. **They** were looking for the teacher.	A plural pronoun is used to refer to a plural noun, as in (c).
(d) **A student** should always do **his** assignments.	With a "generic noun"* (e.g, in (d): **a student** = *anyone who is a student*) a singular masculine pronoun has been used traditionally, but many English speakers now use both masculine and feminine pronouns, as in (e).
(e) **A student** should always do **his/her** assignments. **A student** should always do **his or her** assignments.	

*A generic noun does not refer to any person or thing in particular; rather, it represents a whole group. (See Appendix 1, Chart D-1, *Basic Article Usage*.)

5-17 PERSONAL PRONOUNS: AGREEMENT WITH INDEFINITE PRONOUNS

The following are indefinite pronouns:			
everyone	*someone*	*anyone*	*no one*
everybody	*somebody*	*anybody*	*nobody*
everything	*something*	*anything*	*nothing*

(f) **Somebody** left **his** book on the desk.	A singular personal pronoun is used in formal English to refer to an indefinite pronoun, as in (f) and (g).
(g) **Everyone** has **his or her** own ideas.	
(h) INFORMAL: **Somebody** left **their** book on the desk. **Everyone** has **their** own ideas.	In everyday informal English, a plural personal pronoun is often used to refer to an indefinite pronoun, as in (h).

5-18 PERSONAL PRONOUNS: AGREEMENT WITH COLLECTIVE NOUNS

The following are examples of collective nouns:	
audience couple family public class crowd government staff committee faculty group team	
(a) *My family* is large. *It* is composed of nine members.	When a collective noun refers to a single impersonal unit, a singular pronoun (*it, its*) is used, as in (a).
(b) *My family* is loving and supportive. *They* are always ready to help me.	When a collective noun refers to a collection of various individuals, a plural pronoun (*they, them, their*) is used, as in (b).★

★NOTE: When the collective noun refers to a collection of individuals, the verb may be either singular or plural: *My family **is** OR **are** loving and supportive.* A singular verb is generally preferred in American English. A plural verb is used more frequently in British English, especially with the words *government* and *public.* (American: **The government is** *planning many changes.* British: **The government are** *planning many changes.*)

5-19 USING REFLEXIVE PRONOUNS

The following are reflexive pronouns:	
myself ourselves yourself yourselves himself, herself, itself themselves	
(a) *He* looked at *himself* in the mirror.	A reflexive pronoun usually refers to the subject of a sentence. In (a): *he* and *himself* refer to the same person.
(b) *He himself* answered the phone, not his secretary. (c) *He* answered the phone *himself*.	Sometimes reflexive pronouns are used for emphasis, as in (b) and (c).
(d) She lives *by herself*.	The expression *by + a reflexive pronoun* usually means "alone," as in (d).

Bob is looking at *himself* in the mirror.

Jane is looking at *herself*.

They are looking at *themselves*.

5–20 USING *YOU* AND *ONE* AS IMPERSONAL PRONOUNS

(a) **One** should always be polite. (b) How does **one** get to 5th Avenue from here?	In (a) and (b): **one** means "any person, people in general." In (c) and (d): **you** means "any person, people in general."
(c) **You** should always be polite. (d) How do **you** get to 5th Avenue from here?	**One** is more formal than **you**. Impersonal **you**, rather than **one**, is used more frequently in everyday English.

(e) **One** should take care of **one's** health.
    One should take care of **his** health.
    One should take care of **his or her** health.
	In (e): Notice the pronouns that may be used in the same sentence to refer back to **one**.

5–21 FORMS OF *OTHER*

	ADJECTIVE	PRONOUN	
singular: *plural:*	**another book (is)** **other books (are)**	**another (is)** **others (are)**	Forms of **other** are used as either adjectives or pronouns. Notice: A final **-s** is used only for a plural pronoun (**others**).
singular: *plural:*	**the other book (is)** **the other books (are)**	**the other (is)** **the others (are)**	

(a) The students in the class come from many countries. One of the students is from Mexico. **Another student is** from Iraq. **Another is** from Japan. **Other students are** from Brazil. **Others are** from Algeria.	The meaning of **another**: *one more in addition to the one(s) already mentioned.* The meaning of **other/others** (without *the*): *several more in addition to the one(s) already mentioned.*
(b) I have three books. Two are mine. **The other book** is yours. (**The other** is yours.) (c) I have three books. One is mine. **The other books** are yours. (**The others** are yours.)	The meaning of **the other(s)**: *all that remains from a given number; the rest of a specific group.*
(d) We write to **each other** every week. (e) We write to **one another** every week.	**Each other** and **one another** indicate a reciprocal relationship. In (d) and (e): I write to him every week, and he writes to me every week.

(f) Please write on **every other** *line*.
(g) I see her **every other** *week*.
	Every other can give the idea of "alternate." In (f):
	    Write on the first line.
	    Do not write on the second line.
	    Write on the third line.
	    Do not write on the fourth line.
	    (etc.)

(h) I will be here for **another three years**. (i) I need **another five dollars**. (j) We drove **another ten miles**.	**Another** is used with expressions of time, money, and distance, even if these expressions contain plural nouns.

CHAPTER **6**

Adjective Clauses

6–1 ADJECTIVE CLAUSES: INTRODUCTION

Terms:	**clause:**	*A clause* is a group of words containing a subject and a verb.
	independent clause:	*An independent clause* is a complete sentence. It contains the main subject and verb of a sentence. (It is also called *a main clause*.)
	dependent clause:	*A dependent clause* is not a complete sentence. It must be connected to an independent clause.
	adjective clause:	*An adjective clause* is a dependent clause that modifies a noun. It describes, identifies, or gives further information about a noun. (An adjective clause is also called *a relative clause*.)

6–2 USING SUBJECT PRONOUNS: *WHO, WHICH, THAT*

I thanked the woman. ***She*** helped me. ↓ (a) I thanked the woman ***who*** *helped me.* (b) I thanked the woman ***that*** *helped me.*	In (a): *I thanked the woman* = an independent clause *who helped me* = an adjective clause The adjective clause modifies the noun *woman*.
	In (a): ***who*** is the subject of the adjective clause. In (b): ***that*** is the subject of the adjective clause. Note: (a) and (b) have the same meaning.
The book is mine. ***It*** is on the table. ↓ (c) The book ***which*** *is on the table* is mine. (d) The book ***that*** *is on the table* is mine.	***who*** = used for people ***which*** = used for things ***that*** = used for both people and things

NOTE: In everday usage, often one pattern is used more commonly than another:
    (1) As a subject pronoun, ***who*** is more common than ***that***.
    (2) As a subject pronoun, ***that*** is more common than ***which***.

6–3 USING OBJECT PRONOUNS: *WHO(M)*, *WHICH*, *THAT*

1. PRONOUN USED AS THE OBJECT OF A VERB

The man was Mr. Jones.
I saw **him**.

(e) The man   ***who(m)***   *I saw*   was Mr. Jones.
(f) The man   ***that***   *I saw*   was Mr. Jones.
(g) The man   Ø   *I saw*   was Mr. Jones.

The movie wasn't very good.
We saw **it** last night.

(h) The movie   ***which***   *we saw last night*   wasn't very good.
(i) The movie   ***that***   *we saw last night*   wasn't very good.
(j) The movie   Ø   *we saw last night*   wasn't very good.

Notice in the examples: The adjective clause pronouns are placed at the *beginning* of the clause. (General guideline: Place an adjective clause pronoun as close as possible to the noun it modifies.)

In (e): ***who*** is usually used instead of ***whom***, especially in speaking. ***Whom*** is generally used only in very formal English.

In (g) and (j): An object pronoun is often omitted from an adjective clause. (A subject pronoun, however, may not be omitted.)

who(m) = used for people
which = used for things
that = used for both people and things

2. PRONOUN USED AS THE OBJECT OF A PREPOSITION

She is the woman.
I told you **about her**.

(k) She is the woman   ***about whom***   *I told you*.
(l) She is the woman   ***who(m)***   *I told you **about***.
(m) She is the woman   ***that***   *I told you **about***.
(n) She is the woman   Ø   *I told you **about***.

The music was good.
We listened **to it** last night.

(o) The music   ***to which***   *we listened*   *last night*   was good.
(p) The music   ***which***   *we listened **to***   *last night*   was good.
(q) The music   ***that***   *we listened **to***   *last night*   was good.
(r) The music   Ø   *we listened **to***   *last night*   was good.

In very formal English, the preposition comes at the beginning of the adjective clause, as in (k) and (o). Usually, however, in everyday usage, the preposition comes after the subject and verb of the adjective clause, as in the other examples.

Note: If the preposition comes at the beginning of the adjective clause, only ***whom*** or ***which*** may be used. A preposition is never immediately followed by ***that*** or ***who***.

The woman *I was dancing with* stepped on my toe.

6-4 USING *WHOSE*

I know the man. **His bicycle** was stolen. ↓ (s) I know the man **whose bicycle was stolen**. The student writes well. I read **her composition**. ↓ (t) The student **whose composition I read** writes well.	**Whose** is used to show possession. It carries the same meaning as other possessive pronouns used as adjectives: *his, her, its,* and *their*. Like *his, her, its,* and *their*, **whose** is connected to a noun: *his bicycle* → *whose bicycle* *her composition* → *whose composition* Both **whose** and the noun it is connected to are placed at the beginning of the adjective clause. **Whose** cannot be omitted.
Mr. Catt has a painting. ***Its value*** is inestimable. (u) Mr. Catt has a painting ***whose value*** is inestimable.	**Whose** usually modifies "people," but it may also be used to modify "things," as in (u).

The man's beard caught on fire.
His beard caught on fire when he lit a cigarette.
The man poured a glass of water on his face.

The man **whose beard** caught on fire when he lit
a cigarette poured a glass of water on his face.

6-5 USING *WHERE*

	The building is very old. He lives **there** (**in that building**).		**Where** is used in an adjective clause to modify a place (*city, country, room, house, etc.*).
(a) The building	**where**	*he lives*	is very old.
(b) The building	**in which**	*he lives*	is very old.
The building	**which**	*he lives* **in**	is very old.
The building	**that**	*he lives* **in**	is very old.
The building	Ø	*he lives* **in**	is very old.

Where is used in an adjective clause to modify a place (*city, country, room, house, etc.*).
If **where** is used, a preposition is not included in the adjective clause. If **where** is not used, the preposition must be included.

6–6 USING *WHEN*

	I'll never forget the day. I met you ***then*** (***on that day***).		***When*** is used in an adjective clause to modify a noun of time (*year*, *day*, *time*, *century*, etc.)
(c) I'll never forget the day	***when***	*I met you.*	
(d) I'll never forget the day	***on which***	*I met you.*	The use of a preposition in an adjective clause that modifies a noun of time is somewhat different from that in other adjective clauses: A preposition is used preceding ***which***, as in (d). Otherwise, the preposition is omitted.
(e) I'll never forget the day	***that***	*I met you.*	
(f) I'll never forget the day	Ø	*I met you.*	

6–7 USING ADJECTIVE CLAUSES TO MODIFY PRONOUNS

(a) There is ***someone*** (*whom*) *I want you to meet.* (b) ***Everything*** *he said* was pure nonsense. (c) ***Anybody*** *who wants to come* is welcome.	Adjective clauses can modify indefinite pronouns (e.g., *someone, everybody*). Object pronouns (e.g., *whom, which*) are usually omitted in the adjective clause.
(d) Paula was ***the only one*** *I knew at the party.* (e) Scholarships are available for ***those*** *who need financial assistance.*	Adjective clauses can modify ***the one(s)*** and ***those***.*
(f) It is ***I*** *who am responsible.* (g) ***He*** *who laughs last* laughs best.	Adjective clauses rarely modify personal pronouns. (f) is very formal and uncommon. (g) is a well-known saying in which ''he'' is used as an indefinite pronoun (meaning ''anyone,'' ''any person'').

*An adjective clause with ***which*** can also be used to modify the pronoun ***that***. For example:
   We sometimes fear ***that which*** *we do not understand.*
   The bread my mother makes is much better than ***that which*** *you can buy at a store.*

There are two goats outside Mrs. Clark's house. She's angry at ***the one*** *that is eating her flowers* but not at ***the one*** *that stayed on the other side of the fence.*

General guidelines for the punctuation of adjective clauses:
    (1) DO NOT USE COMMAS IF the adjective clause is necessary to identify the noun it modifies.*
    (2) USE COMMAS IF the adjective clause simply gives additional information and is not necessary to identify the noun it modifies.**

(a) **The professor** who teaches Chemistry 101 is an excellent lecturer.	In (a): No commas are used. The adjective clause is necessary to identify which professor is meant.
(b) **Professor Wilson**, who teaches Chemistry 101, is an excellent lecturer.	In (b): Commas are used. The adjective clause is not necessary to identify who Professor Wilson is. We already know who he is: he has a name. The adjective clause simply gives additional information.
(c) **Hawaii**, which consists of eight principal islands, is a favorite vacation spot. (d) **Mrs. Smith**, who is a retired teacher, does volunteer work at the hospital.	Guideline: Use commas, as in (b), (c), and (d), if an adjective clause modifies a proper noun. (A proper noun begins with a capital letter, not a small letter.) Note: A comma reflects a pause in speech.
(e) **The man** { who(m) / that / ∅ } I met teaches chemistry. (f) **Mr. Lee**, whom I met yesterday, teaches chemistry.	In (e): If no commas are used, any possible pronoun may be used in the adjective clause. Object pronouns may be omitted. In (f): When commas are necessary, the pronoun **that** may not be used (only **who, whom, which, whose, where,** and **when** may be used), and object pronouns cannot be omitted.
COMPARE THE MEANING (g) We took some children on a picnic. **The children, who wanted to play soccer,** ran to an open field as soon as we arrived at the park. (h) We took some children on a picnic. **The children who wanted to play soccer** ran to an open field as soon as we arrived at the park. The others played a different game.	In (g): The use of commas means that *all* of the children wanted to play soccer and all of the children ran to an open field. The adjective clause is used only to give additional information about the children. In (h): The lack of commas means that *only some* of the children wanted to play soccer. The adjective clause is used to identify which children ran to the open field.

*Adjective clauses that do not require commas are called "essential" or "restrictive" or "identifying."
**Adjective clauses that require commas are called "nonessential" or "nonrestrictive" or "nonidentifying."
  Note: Nonessential adjective clauses are more common in writing than in speaking.

76

6-9 USING EXPRESSIONS OF QUANTITY IN ADJECTIVE CLAUSES

In my class there are 20 students. *Most of them* are from the Far East. (a) In my class there are 20 students, *most of whom* are from the Far East.	An adjective clause may contain an expression of quantity with *of*: *some of, many of, most of, none of, two of, half of, both of, neither of, each of, all of, both of, several of, a few of, little of, a number of,* etc.
He gave several reasons. *Only a few of them* were valid. (b) He gave several reasons, *only a few of which* were valid.	The expression of quantity precedes the pronoun. Only *whom, which,* and *whose* are used in this pattern.
The teachers discussed Jim. *One of his problems* was poor study habits. (c) The teachers discussed Jim, *one of whose problems* was poor study habits.	Adjective clauses that begin with an expression of quantity are more common in writing than speaking. Commas are used.

6-10 USING *NOUN + OF WHICH*

We have an antique table. *The top of it* has jade inlay. (a) We have an antique table, *the top of which* has jade inlay.	An adjective clause may include *a noun + of which* (e.g., *the top of which*). This pattern carries the meaning of *whose* (e.g., We have *an antique table whose top has jade inlay.*). This pattern is used in an adjective clause that modifies a "thing" and occurs primarily in formal written English. Commas are used.

6-11 USING *WHICH* TO MODIFY A WHOLE SENTENCE

(a) Tom was late. (b) *That* surprised me. (c) Tom was late, *which surprised me.*	The pronouns *that* and *this* can refer to the idea of a whole sentence which comes before. In (b): The word *that* refers to the whole sentence "Tom was late."
(d) The elevator is out of order. (e) *This* is too bad. (f) The elevator is out of order, *which is too bad.*	Similarly, an adjective clause with *which* may modify the idea of a whole sentence. In (c): The word *which* refers to the whole sentence "Tom was late."*

*Using *which* to modify a whole sentence is informal and occurs most frequently in spoken English. This structure is generally not appropriate in formal writing. Whenever it is written, however, it is preceded by a comma to reflect a pause in speech.

6-12 REDUCTION OF ADJECTIVE CLAUSES TO ADJECTIVE PHRASES: INTRODUCTION

Terms: **clause:** *A clause* is a group of related words that contains a subject and a verb. **phrase:** *A phrase* is a group of related words that does not contain a subject and a verb.	

(a) ADJECTIVE CLAUSE:
  The girl ***who is sitting next to me*** is Mary.
 (b) ADJECTIVE PHRASE:
  The girl ***sitting next to me*** is Mary.
	An adjective phrase is a reduction of an adjective clause. It modifies a noun. It does not contain a subject and a verb. The adjective clause in (a) can be reduced to the adjective phrase in (b). (a) and (b) have the same meaning.

(c) CLAUSE: The boy ***who is playing the piano*** is Ben. (d) PHRASE: The boy ***playing the piano*** is Ben. (e) CLAUSE: The boy ***(whom) I saw*** was Tom. (f) PHRASE: *(none)*	Only adjective clauses that have a subject pronoun—***who***, ***which***, or ***that***—are reduced to modifying adjective phrases. The adjective clause in (e) cannot be reduced to an adjective phrase.

6-13 CHANGING AN ADJECTIVE CLAUSE TO AN ADJECTIVE PHRASE

There are two ways in which an adjective clause is changed to an adjective phrase:

(1) The subject pronoun is omitted AND the ***be*** form of the verb is omitted.
  (a) CLAUSE: The ***man who is talking*** to John is from Korea.
   PHRASE: The ***man*** Ø Ø ***talking*** to John is from Korea.
  (b) CLAUSE: The ***ideas which are presented*** in that book are interesting.
   PHRASE: The ***ideas*** Ø Ø ***presented*** in that book are interesting.
  (c) CLAUSE: Ann is the ***woman who is responsible*** for preparing the budget.
   PHRASE: Ann is the ***woman*** Ø Ø ***responsible*** for preparing the budget.
  (d) CLAUSE: The ***books that are on that shelf*** are mine.
   PHRASE: The ***books*** Ø Ø ***on that shelf*** are mine.

(2) If there is no ***be*** form of a verb in the adjective clause, it is sometimes possible to omit the subject pronoun and change the verb to its ***-ing*** form.
  (e) CLAUSE: English has an ***alphabet that consists*** of 26 letters.
   PHRASE: English has an ***alphabet*** Ø ***consisting*** of 26 letters.
  (f) CLAUSE: ***Anyone who wants*** to come with us is welcome.
   PHRASE: ***Anyone*** Ø ***wanting*** to come with us is welcome.

(g) *George Washington*, *who was the first president of the United States*, was a wealthy colonist and a general in the army. (h) *George Washington*, *the first president of the United States*, was a wealthy colonist and a general in the army.	If the adjective clause requires commas, as in (g), the adjective phrase also requires commas, as in (h).

CHAPTER *7*

Noun Clauses

7–1 NOUN CLAUSES: INTRODUCTION

A *noun* is used as a subject or an object.

A *noun clause* is used as a subject or an object. In other words, a noun clause is used in the same ways as a noun.

(a) **His story** was interesting. (b) **What he said** was interesting.	In (a): **story** is a noun. It is used as the subject of the sentence. In (b): **what he said** is a noun clause. It is used as the subject of the sentence. The noun clause has its own subject (*he*) and verb (*said*).
(c) I heard **his story**. (d) I heard **what he said**.	In (c): **story** is a noun. It is used as the object of the verb **heard**. In (d): **what he said** is a noun clause. It is used as the object of the verb **heard**.

WORDS USED TO INTRODUCE NOUN CLAUSES

(1) *question words:**
when	*who*
where	*whom*
why	*what*
how	*which*
	whose

(2) *whether*
   if

(3) *that*

*See Appendix 1, Unit B, for more information about question words and question forms.

7–2 NOUN CLAUSES WHICH BEGIN WITH A QUESTION WORD

QUESTION	NOUN CLAUSE	
QUESTION Where does she live? What did he say? When do they arrive?	**NOUN CLAUSE** (a) I don't know *where she lives*. (b) I couldn't hear *what he said*. (c) Do you know *when they arrive*?	In (a): *where she lives* is the object of the verb *know*. Do not use question word order in a noun clause. In a noun clause, the subject precedes the verb. Notice: *does*, *did*, and *do* are used in questions but not in noun clauses.
s v Who lives there? What happened? Who is at the door?	s v (d) I don't know *who lives there*. (e) Please tell me *what happened*. (f) I wonder *who is at the door*.	In (d): The word order is the same in both the question and the noun clause because *who* is the subject in both.
v s Who is she? Who are those men? Whose house is that?	s v (g) I don't know *who she is*. (h) I don't know *who those men are*. (i) I wonder *whose house that is*.	In (g): *she* is the subject of the question, so it is placed in front of the verb *be* in the noun clause.*
What did she say? What should they do?	(j) **What she said** surprised me. (k) **What they should do** is obvious.	In (j): **what she said** is the subject of the sentence. Notice in (k): A noun clause subject takes a singular verb (e.g., *is*).

*COMPARE: *Who is at the door?* = *who* is the subject of the question.
              Who are those men? = *those men* is the subject of the question, so *be* is plural.

7–3 NOUN CLAUSES WHICH BEGIN WITH *WHETHER* OR *IF*

YES/NO QUESTION	NOUN CLAUSE	

YES/NO QUESTION
Will she come?
 	
Does he need help?
	NOUN CLAUSE
	(a) I don't know *whether she will come*.
	    I don't know *if she will come*.
	(b) I wonder *whether he needs help*.
	    I wonder *if he needs help*.
	(c) I wonder *whether or not* she will come.
	(d) I wonder *whether* she will come *or not*.
	(e) I wonder *if* she will come *or not*.
		When a yes/no question is changed to a noun clause, *whether* or *if* is used to introduce the clause.
		(Note: *whether* is more acceptable in formal English, but *if* is quite commonly used, especially in speaking.)
		In (c), (d), and (e): Notice the patterns when *or not* is used.

	(f) **Whether she comes or not** is unimportant to me.	In (f): Notice that the noun clause is in the subject position.

7-4 QUESTION WORDS FOLLOWED BY INFINITIVES

(a) I don't know *what I should do*. (b) I don't know ***what to do***. (c) Pam can't decide *whether she should go or stay home*. (d) Pam can't decide ***whether to go or (to) stay home***. (e) Please tell me *how I can get to the bus station*. (f) Please tell me ***how to get to the bus station***. (g) Jim told us *where we could find it*. (h) Jim told us ***where to find it***.	Question words (***when, where, how, who, whom, whose, what, which***) and ***whether*** may be followed by an infinitive. Each pair of sentences in the examples has the same meaning. Notice that the meaning expressed by the infinitive is either ***should*** or ***can/could***.

7-5 NOUN CLAUSES WHICH BEGIN WITH *THAT*

STATEMENT *(Expression of an idea or fact)*	NOUN CLAUSE	
He is a good actor. The world is round.	(a) I think ***that he is a good actor***. (b) I think ***he is a good actor***. (c) We know ***(that) the world is round***.	In (a): ***that he is a good actor*** is a noun clause. It is used as the object of the verb ***think***. The word ***that***, when it introduces a noun clause, has no meaning in itself. It simply marks the beginning of the clause. Frequently it is omitted, as in (b), especially in speaking. (If used in speaking, it is unstressed.)
She doesn't understand spoken English. The world is round.	(d) ***That*** *she doesn't understand spoken English* is obvious. (e) ***It*** is obvious *(**that**) she doesn't understand spoken English*. (f) ***That*** *the world is round* is a fact. (g) ***It*** is a fact ***that*** *the world is round*.	In (d): The noun clause (***That she doesn't understand spoken English***) is used as the subject of the sentence. The word ***that*** is not omitted when it introduces a noun clause used as the subject of a sentence, as in (d) and (f). More commonly, the word ***it*** functions as the subject, and the noun clause is placed at the end of the sentence, as in (e) and (g).

7-6 QUOTED SPEECH*

Quoted speech refers to reproducing words exactly as they were originally spoken. Quotation marks (". . .") are used.**	

QUOTING ONE SENTENCE	In (a): Use a comma after **she said**. Capitalize the first word of the quoted sentence. Put the final quotation marks outside of the period at the end of the sentence.
(a) She said, "My brother is a student."	
(b) "My brother is a student," she said.	In (b): Use a comma, not a period, at the end of the quoted sentence when it precedes **she said**.
(c) "My brother," she said, "is a student."	In (c): If the quoted sentence is divided by **she said**, use a comma after the first part of the quote. Do not capitalize the first word of the second half of the quoted sentence.
QUOTING MORE THAN ONE SENTENCE	In (d): Quotation marks are placed at the beginning and end of the complete quote. Notice: There are no quotation marks after **student**.
(d) "My brother is a student. He is attending a university," she said.	
QUOTING A QUESTION OR AN EXCLAMATION	In (e): The question mark is inside the quotation marks.
(e) She asked, "When will you be here?"	
(f) "When will you be here?" she asked.	In (f): If a question mark is used, no comma is used before **she asked**.
(g) She said, "Watch out!"	In (g): The exclamation point is inside the quotation marks.

Quoted speech is also called *direct speech*. *Reported speech* (discussed in Chart 7–7) is also called *indirect speech*.
**In British English, quotation marks are called *inverted commas*.

"What's wrong, Officer?" I asked. "Was I speeding?"

"No, you weren't speeding," he replied. "You went through a red light."

"Did I really do that?" I said. "I didn't see the red light."

"Your driver's license, please."

7-7 REPORTED SPEECH AND THE FORMAL SEQUENCE OF TENSES IN NOUN CLAUSES

Reported speech refers to using a noun clause to report what someone has said. No quotation marks are used. Notice the changes in the verb forms from quoted speech to reported speech in the following examples.

QUOTED SPEECH		REPORTED SPEECH
(a) She said, "I *watch* TV every day."	→	She said (that) she *watched* TV every day.
(b) She said, "I *am watching* TV."	→	She said she *was watching* TV.
(c) She said, "I *have watched* TV."	→	She said she *had watched* TV.
(d) She said, "I *watched* TV."	→	She said she *had watched* TV.
(e) She said, "I *will watch* TV."	→	She said she *would watch* TV.
(f) She said, "I *am going to watch* TV."	→	She said she *was going to watch* TV.
(g) She said, "I *can watch* TV."	→	She said she *could watch* TV.
(h) She said, "I *may watch* TV."	→	She said she *might watch* TV.
(i) She said, "I *might watch* TV."	→	She said she *might watch* TV.
(j) She said, "I *must watch* TV."	→	She said she *had to watch* TV.
(k) She said, "I *have to watch* TV."	→	She said she *had to watch* TV.
(l) She said, "I *should watch* TV."	→	She said she *should watch* TV.
(m) She said, "I *ought to watch* TV."	→	She said she *ought to watch* TV.
(n) She said, "*Watch* TV."	→	She *told me to watch* TV.*
(o) She said, "*Do* you *watch* TV?"	→	She *asked (me) if* I *watched* TV.

GENERAL GUIDELINES ON TENSE USAGE IN A NOUN CLAUSE

(1) If the reporting verb (the main verb of the sentence, e.g., *said*) is in the past, the verb in the noun clause will usually also be in a past form.

(2) This formal sequence of tenses in noun clauses is used in both speaking and writing. However, sometimes in spoken English, no change is made in the noun clause verb, especially if the speaker is reporting something immediately or soon after it was said.

Immediate reporting: A: *What did the teacher just say? I didn't hear him.*
                       B: *He said he **wants** us to read Chapter Six.*

Later reporting: A: *I didn't go to class yesterday. Did Mr. Jones make any assignments?*
                  B: *Yes. He said he **wanted** us to read Chapter Six.*

(3) Also, sometimes the present tense is retained even in formal English when the reported sentence deals with a general truth: *She said that the world **is** round.*

(4) When the reporting verb is simple present, present perfect, or future, the noun clause verb is not changed.

She *says*, "I *watch* TV every day."	→	She *says* she *watches* TV every day.
She *has said*, "I *watch* TV every day."	→	She *has said* that she *watches* TV every day.
She *will say*, "I *watch* TV every day."	→	She *will say* that she *watches* TV every day.

*In reported speech, an imperative sentence is changed to an infinitive. *Tell* is used instead of *say* as the reporting verb. (See Chart 4-5 for other verbs followed by an infinitive that are used to report speech.) Also note that *tell* is immediately followed by a (pro)noun object, but *say* is not:

*He told **me** he would be late. He said he would be late.* Also possible: *He said **to me** he would be late.*

7-8 USING THE SUBJUNCTIVE IN NOUN CLAUSES

(a) The teacher **demands** that we **be** on time. (b) I **insisted** that he **pay** me the money. (c) I **recommended** that she **not go** to the concert. (d) **It is important** that they **be told** the truth.	In (a): **be** is a subjunctive verb. The subjunctive is used in a noun clause that follows certain verbs and expressions. The sentences generally *stress importance*. In these sentences, the subjunctive verb is used only in its simple form. It does not have present, past, or future form; it is neither singular nor plural. Negative: **not** + *simple form*, as in (c). Passive: simple form of **be** + *past participle*, as in (d).
(e) I **suggested** that she **see** a doctor. (f) I **suggested** that she **should see** a doctor.	**Should** is also possible after **suggest** and **recommend**.*

COMMON VERBS AND EXPRESSIONS FOLLOWED BY THE SUBJUNCTIVE IN A NOUN CLAUSE

demand (that)	suggest (that)	it is important (that)
insist (that)	recommend (that)	it is necessary (that)
request (that)	advise (that)	it is essential (that)
ask (that)	propose (that)	it is vital (that)
		it is imperative (that)

*The subjunctive is more common in American English than British English. In British English, **should** + *simple form* is more usual than the subjunctive: e.g., The teacher **insists** that we **should be** on time.

7-9 USING -*EVER* WORDS

The following -*ever* words give the idea of "any." Each pair of sentences in the examples has the same meaning.

whoever	(a)	**Whoever** wants to come is welcome. *Anyone who* wants to come is welcome.
who(m)ever	(b)	He makes friends easily with **who(m)ever** he meets.* He makes friends easily with *anyone who(m)* he meets.
whatever	(c)	He always says **whatever** comes into his mind. He always says *anything that* comes into his mind.
whichever	(d)	There are four good programs on TV at eight o'clock. We can watch **whichever program (whichever one)** you prefer. We can watch *any of the four programs that* you prefer.
whenever	(e)	You may leave **whenever** you wish. You may leave *at any time that* you wish.
wherever	(f)	She can go **wherever** she wants to go. She can go *anyplace that* she wants to go.
however	(g)	The students may dress **however** they please. The students may dress *in any way that* they please.

*In (b): **whomever** is the object of the verb **meets**. In American English, **whomever** is rare and very formal. In British English, **whoever** (not **whomever**) is used as the object form: He makes friends easily with whoever he meets.

CHAPTER 8
Showing Relationships Between Ideas—Part I

8–1 PARALLEL STRUCTURE

<table>
<tr>
<td colspan="2">One use of a conjunction is to connect words or phrases that have the same grammatical function in a sentence. This use of conjunctions is called parallel structure. The conjunctions used in this pattern are: and, but, or, nor.★</td>
</tr>
<tr>
<td>(a) Steve and his friend are coming to dinner.</td>
<td>In (a): noun + and + noun</td>
</tr>
<tr>
<td>(b) Susan raised her hand and snapped her fingers.</td>
<td>In (b): verb + and + verb</td>
</tr>
<tr>
<td>(c) He is waving his arms and (is) shouting at us.</td>
<td>In (c): verb + and + verb (The second auxiliary may be omitted if it is the same as the first auxiliary.)</td>
</tr>
<tr>
<td>(d) These shoes are old but comfortable.</td>
<td>In (d): adjective + but + adjective</td>
</tr>
<tr>
<td>(e) He wants to watch TV or (to) listen to some music.</td>
<td>In (e): infinitive + or + infinitive (The second to may be omitted.)</td>
</tr>
<tr>
<td>(f) Steve, Joe, and Alice are coming to dinner.</td>
<td rowspan="3">A parallel structure may contain more than two parts. In a series, commas are used to separate each unit. The final comma that precedes the conjunction is optional but is customarily used. (No commas are used if there are only two parts to a parallel structure.)</td>
</tr>
<tr>
<td>(g) Susan raised her hand, snapped her fingers, and asked a question.</td>
</tr>
<tr>
<td>(h) The colors in that fabric are red, gold, black, and green.</td>
</tr>
</table>

★More specifically, **and, but, or, nor** are called *coordinating conjunctions*.

Eric gave Amy *flowers* on Sunday, *candy* on Monday, **and** *a ring* on Tuesday.

8-2 USING PAIRED CONJUNCTIONS: *BOTH . . . AND; NOT ONLY . . . BUT ALSO; EITHER . . . OR; NEITHER . . . NOR*★

(a) **Both my mother and my sister** *are* here. (b) **Not only my mother but also my sister** *is* here. (c) **Not only my sister but also my parents** *are* here. (d) **Neither my mother nor my sister** *is* here. (e) **Neither my sister nor my parents** *are* here.	Two subjects connected by **both** . . . **and** take a plural verb. When two subjects are connected by **not only** . . . **but also**, **either** . . . **or**, or **neither** . . . **nor**, the subject that is closer to the verb determines whether the verb is singular or plural.
(f) The research project will take **both** *time* **and** *money*. (g) Yesterday it **not only** *rained* **but (also)** *snowed*. (h) I'll take **either** *chemistry* **or** *physics* next quarter. (i) That book is **neither** *interesting* **nor** *accurate*.	Notice the parallel structure in the examples. The *same* grammatical form should follow each word of the pair. In (f): **both** + *noun* + **and** + *noun* In (g): **not only** + *verb* + **but also** + *verb* In (h): **either** + *noun* + **or** + *noun* In (i): **neither** + *adjective* + **nor** + *adjective*

★Paired conjunctions are also called *correlative conjunctions*.

Fred **not only** *fed* the baby **but also** *burped* him.

Both Fred *and* the baby **look** unhappy.
Neither Fred *nor* the baby **looks** happy.

(a) It was raining hard. There was a strong wind. (b) *INCORRECT PUNCTUATION:* It was raining hard, there was a strong wind.	Example (a) contains two independent clauses (i.e., two complete sentences). Notice the punctuation. A period,* NOT A COMMA, is used to separate two independent clauses. The punctuation in (b) is not correct; the error in (b) is called *a run-on sentence*.
(c) It was raining hard, **and** there was a strong wind. (d) It was raining hard **and** there was a strong wind. (e) It was raining hard. **And** there was a strong wind.	A conjunction may be used to connect two independent clauses. *Punctuation:* In (c): Usually a comma immediately precedes the conjunction. In (d): Sometimes in short sentences the comma is omitted. In (e): Sometimes in informal writing a conjunction may begin a sentence.
(f) He was tired, **so** he went to bed. (g) The child hid behind his mother's skirt, **for** he was afraid of the dog. (h) He did not study, **yet** he passed the exam.	In addition to **and**, **but**, **or**, and **nor**, other conjunctions are used to connect two independent clauses: **so** (meaning *therefore, as a result*) **for** (meaning *because*) **yet** (meaning *but, nevertheless*) A comma almost always precedes **so**, **for**, and **yet** when they are used as conjunctions.**

*In British English, *a period* is called *a full stop*.

So, for*, and *yet* have other meanings in other structures: e.g., *He is not so tall as his brother.* (so** = **as**)   *We waited for the bus.* (**for** = a preposition)   *She hasn't arrived yet.* (**yet** = an adverb meaning *up to this time*).

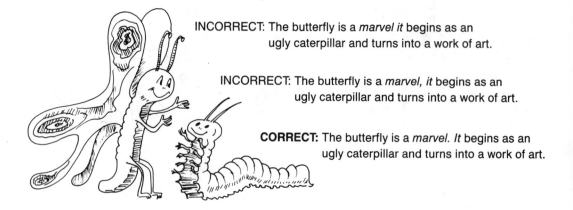

INCORRECT: The butterfly is a *marvel it* begins as an ugly caterpillar and turns into a work of art.

INCORRECT: The butterfly is a *marvel, it* begins as an ugly caterpillar and turns into a work of art.

CORRECT: The butterfly is a *marvel. It* begins as an ugly caterpillar and turns into a work of art.

8–4 ADVERB CLAUSES: INTRODUCTION

(a) ***When we were in New York***, we saw several plays. (b) We saw several plays ***when we were in New York***.	***When we were in New York*** is an adverb clause. It is a dependent clause. It cannot stand alone as a sentence. It must be connected to an independent clause. *Punctuation:* When an adverb clause precedes an independent clause, as in (a), a comma is used to separate the clauses. When the adverb clause follows, as in (b), usually no comma is used.
(c) ***Because he was sleepy***, he went to bed. (d) He went to bed ***because he was sleepy***.	Like ***when***, ***because*** introduces an adverb clause. ***Because he was sleepy*** is an adverb clause.

SUMMARY LIST OF WORDS USED TO INTRODUCE ADVERB CLAUSES★

TIME	CAUSE AND EFFECT	OPPOSITION	CONDITION
after	*because*	*even though*	*if*
before	*since*	*although*	*unless*
when	*now that*	*though*	*only if*
while	*as*		*whether or not*
as	*as/so long as*		*even if*
by the time (that)	*inasmuch as*	*whereas*	*providing (that)*
since		*while*	*provided (that)*
until			*in case (that)*
as soon as	*so (that)*		*in the event (that)*
once	*in order that*		
as/so long as			
whenever			
every time (that)			
the first time (that)			
the last time (that)			
the next time (that)			

★Words that introduce adverb clauses are called *subordinating conjunctions*.

- Jane's contact lens popped out ***while*** *she was playing basketball.*

- ***If*** *a player loses a contact lens*, the referees stop a game.

- ***When*** *Jane lost her lens*, the game stopped.

- The game stopped ***because*** *Jane lost her contact lens.*

- ***As soon as*** *the game stopped*, Jane and her teammates got on their hands and knees and looked for her contact lens.

8–5 USING ADVERB CLAUSES TO SHOW TIME RELATIONSHIPS

after	(a) **After** *she graduates*, she will get a job. (b) **After** *she (had) graduated*, she got a job.	A present tense, *not* a future tense, is used in an adverb clause of time. Notice examples (b) and (d). (See Chart 1-21 for tense usage in future time clauses.)
before	(c) I will leave **before** *he comes*. (d) I (had) left **before** *he came*.	
when	(e) **When** *I arrived*, he was talking on the phone. (f) **When** *I got there*, he had already left. (g) **When** *it began to rain*, I stood under a tree. (h) **When** *I was in Chicago*, I visited the museums. (i) **When** *I see him tomorrow*, I will ask him.	**when** = *at that time* (Notice the different time relationships expressed by the tenses.
while as	(j) **While** *I was walking home*, it began to rain. (k) **As** *I was walking home*, it began to rain.	**while**, **as** = *during that time*
by the time	(l) **By the time** *he arrived*, we had already left. (m) **By the time** *he comes*, we will already have left.	**by the time** = *one event is completed before another event* (Notice the use of the past perfect and future perfect in the main clause.)
since	(n) I haven't seen him **since** *he left this morning*.	**since** = *from that time to the present* (Notice: The present perfect tense is used in the main clause.
until till	(o) We stayed there **until** *we finished our work*. (p) We stayed there **till** *we finished our work*.	**until**, **till** = *to that time and then no longer* (**Till** is used primarily in speaking rather than writing.)
as soon as once	(q) **As soon as** *it stops raining*, we will leave. (r) **Once** *it stops raining*, we will leave.	**as soon as**, **once** = *when one event happens, another event happens soon afterwards*
as long as so long as	(s) I will never speak to him again **as long as** *I live*. (t) I will never speak to him again **so long as** *I live*.	**as long as**, **so long as** = *during all that time, from beginning to end*
whenever every time	(u) **Whenever** *I see her*, I say hello. (v) **Every time** *I see her*, I say hello.	**whenever** = *every time*
the first time the last time the next time	(w) **The first time** *I went to New York*, I went to an opera. (x) I saw two plays **the last time** *I went to New York*. (y) **The next time** *I go to New York*, I'm going to see a ballet.	Adverb clauses can be introduced by the following: the $\begin{cases} \textbf{first} \\ \textbf{second} \\ \textbf{third} \\ \textbf{last} \\ \textbf{next} \end{cases}$ time

8–5.1   ADVERB CLAUSES WITH *AFTER* AND *AFTERWARD(S)*

(a) *After I ate dinner*, I took a walk. I took a walk *after I ate dinner*.	*After* can be used to introduce an adverb clause.
(b) I ate dinner. *Afterwards*, I took a walk. I ate dinner. *I took a walk **afterwards***.	*Afterward(s)** is an adverb meaning "*later, after that*."

Afterwards* can also be spelled without **-s.

8–6   USING ADVERB CLAUSES TO SHOW CAUSE AND EFFECT RELATIONSHIPS

because	(a) ***Because** he was sleepy*, he went to bed. (b) He went to bed ***because** he was sleepy*.	An adverb clause may precede or follow the independent clause. Notice the punctuation in (a) and (b).
since	(c) ***Since** he's not interested in classical music*, he decided not to go to the concert.	In (c): *since* means *because*.
now that	(d) ***Now that** the semester is finished*, I'm going to rest a few days and then take a trip.	In (d): ***now that*** means *because now*. ***Now that*** is used for present and future situations.
as	(e) ***As** she had nothing in particular to do*, she called up a friend and asked her if she wanted to take in a movie.	In (e): ***as*** means *because*.
as/so long as	(f) ***As long as (So long as)** you're not busy*, could you help me with this work?	In (f): ***as long as*** means *because*.
inasmuch as	(g) ***Inasmuch as** the two government leaders could not reach an agreement*, the possibilities for peace are still remote.	In (g): ***inasmuch as*** means *because*. ***Inasmuch as*** is usually found only in formal writing and speech.

8–7 USING PREPOSITIONS TO SHOW CAUSE AND EFFECT: *BECAUSE OF* AND *DUE TO*

(a) ***Because*** *the weather was cold*, we stayed home.	***Because*** introduces an adverb clause; it is followed by a subject and verb.
(b) ***Because of*** *the cold weather*, we stayed home. (c) ***Due to*** *the cold weather*, we stayed home.	***Because of*** and ***due to*** are prepositions; they are followed by a noun object.
(d) ***Due to the fact that*** *the weather was cold*, we stayed home.	Sometimes, usually in more formal writing, ***due to*** is followed by a noun clause introduced by ***the fact that***.
(e) We stayed home *because of the cold weather*. We stayed home *due to the cold weather*. We stayed home *due to the fact that the weather was cold*.	Like adverb clauses, these phrases can also follow the main clause, as in (e).

8–8 USING TRANSITIONS TO SHOW CAUSE AND EFFECT: *THEREFORE* AND *CONSEQUENTLY*

(a) Al failed the test because he didn't study. (b) Al didn't study. ***Therefore***, he failed the test. (c) Al didn't study. ***Consequently***, he failed the test.	(a), (b), and (c) have the same meaning. ***Therefore*** and ***consequently*** mean "as a result." In grammar, they are called *transitions* (or *conjunctive adverbs*). Transitions connect the ideas between two sentences.
(d) Al didn't study. ***Therefore***, he failed the test. (e) Al didn't study. He, ***therefore***, failed the test. (f) Al didn't study. He failed the test, ***therefore***. **POSITIONS OF A TRANSITION:** **transition** + **S** + **V** (+ rest of sentence) **S** + **transition** + **V** (+ rest of sentence) **S** + **V** (+ rest of sentence) + **transition**	A transition occurs in the second of two related sentences. Notice the patterns and punctuation in the examples. A period (NOT a comma) is used at the end of the first sentence. The transition has several possible positions in the second sentence. The transition is set off from the rest of the sentence by commas.
(g) Al didn't study, ***so*** he failed the test.	COMPARE: A transition (e.g., ***therefore***) has different possible positions within the second sentence of a pair. A conjunction (e.g., ***so***) has only one possible position: between the two sentences. (See Chart 8-3.) ***So*** cannot move around in the second sentence as ***therefore*** can.

8-9 SUMMARY OF PATTERNS AND PUNCTUATION

ADVERB CLAUSE	(a) **Because** *it was hot*, we went swimming. (b) We went swimming *because it was hot*.	An adverb clause may precede or follow an independent clause. *Punctuation:* A comma is used if the adverb clause comes first.
PREPOSITION	(c) **Because of** *the hot weather*, we went swimming. (d) We went swimming **because of** *the hot weather*.	A preposition is followed by a noun object, not by a subject and verb. *Punctuation:* A comma is usually used if the prepositional phrase precedes the subject and verb of the independent clause.
TRANSITION	(e) It was hot. **Therefore**, *we went swimming*. (f) It was hot. *We*, **therefore**, *went swimming*. (g) It was hot. *We went swimming*, **therefore**.	A transition is used with the second sentence of a pair. It shows the relationship of the second idea to the first idea. A transition is movable within the second sentence. *Punctuation:* A period is used between the two independent clauses.★ A comma may NOT be used to separate the clauses. Commas are usually used to set the transition off from the rest of the sentence.
CONJUNCTION	(h) It was hot, **so** *we went swimming*.	A conjunction comes between two independent clauses. *Punctuation:* Usually a comma is used immediately in front of a conjunction.

★A semicolon (;) may be used instead of a period between the two independent clauses.

It was hot; therefore, we went swimming.
It was hot; we, therefore, went swimming.
It was hot; we went swimming, therefore.

In general, a semicolon can be used instead of a period between any two sentences that are closely related in meaning. Example: *Peanuts are not nuts; they are beans.* Notice that a small letter, not a capital letter, immediately follows a semicolon.

The warning signal that his oil might be low flashed on Nick's dashboard. Nick does not know anything about cars or motors. **Therefore**, he stopped at a service station and asked the attendant to check the oil.

8-10 OTHER WAYS OF EXPRESSING CAUSE AND EFFECT: *SUCH . . . THAT* AND *SO . . . THAT*

(a) Because the weather was nice, we went to the zoo. (b) It was *such nice weather that* we went to the zoo. (c) The weather was *so nice that* we went to the zoo.	Examples (a), (b), and (c) have the same meaning.
(d) It was *such good coffee that* I had another cup. (e) It was *such a foggy day that* we couldn't see the road.	*Such . . . that* encloses a modified noun: *such + adjective + noun + that*
(f) The coffee is *so hot that* I can't drink it. (g) I'm *so hungry that* I could eat a horse.	*So . . . that* encloses an adjective or adverb: $$so + \begin{Bmatrix} adjective \\ or \\ adverb \end{Bmatrix} + that$$
(h) She speaks *so fast that* I can't understand her. (i) He walked *so quickly that* I couldn't keep up with him.	
(j) She made *so many mistakes that* she failed the exam. (k) He has *so few friends that* he is always lonely. (l) She has *so much money that* she can buy whatever she wants. (m) He had *so little trouble* with the test *that* he left twenty minutes early.	*So . . . that* is used with *many, few, much,* and *little.*
(n) It was *such a good book* (*that*) I couldn't put it down. (o) I was *so hungry* (*that*) I didn't wait for dinner to eat something.	Sometimes, primarily in speaking, *that* is omitted.

Sally used *so much paper* when she was writing her report *that* the wastepaper basket overflowed.

8–11 EXPRESSING PURPOSE: USING *SO THAT*

(a) I turned off the TV *in order to* enable my roommate to study in peace and quiet.	*In order to* expresses *purpose*. (See Chart 4-10.) In (a): I turned off the TV for a purpose. The purpose was to make it possible for my roommate to study in peace and quiet.
(b) I turned off the TV *so (that)* my roommate could study in peace and quiet.	*So that* also expresses *purpose*.* It expresses the same meaning as *in order to*. The word "that" is often omitted, especially in speaking.
SO THAT + CAN or COULD (c) I'm going to cash a check *so that I can* buy my textbooks.	*So that* is often used instead of *in order to* when the idea of ability is being expressed. *Can* is used in the adverb clause for a present/future meaning. In (c): *so that I can buy* = *in order to be able to buy*.
(d) I cashed a check *so that I could* buy my textbooks.	*Could* is used after *so that* in past sentences.**
SO THAT + WILL/SIMPLE PRESENT or WOULD (e) I'll take my umbrella *so that I won't* get wet. (f) I'll take my umbrella *so that I don't* get wet. (g) Yesterday I took my umbrella *so that I wouldn't* get wet.	In (e): *so that I won't get wet* = *in order to make sure that I won't get wet*. In (f): It is sometimes possible to use the simple present after *so that* in place of *will*; the simple present expresses a future meaning. *Would* is used in past sentences.

*NOTE: *In order that* has the same meaning as *so that* but is less commonly used.

  Example: *I turned off the TV (in order) that my roommate could study in peace and quiet.*

  Both *so that* and *in order that* introduce adverb clauses. It is unusual, but possible, to put these adverb clauses at the beginning of a sentence: *So that my roommate could study in peace and quiet, I turned off the TV.*

**Also possible but less common: the use of *may* or *might* in place of *can* or *could*: e.g., *I cashed a check so that I might buy my textbooks.*

The archeologist found a gold tooth during the excavation of an ancient Egyptian burial site. He used a magnifying glass *so that he could examine the gold tooth carefully.*

8–12 REDUCTION OF ADVERB CLAUSES TO MODIFYING PHRASES: INTRODUCTION

In Chapter 6, we discussed changing adjective clauses to modifying phrases. (See Chart 6-13.) Some adverb clauses may also be changed to modifying phrases, and the ways in which the changes are made are the same:

(1) Omit the subject of the dependent clause and the **be** form of the verb.

    (a) ADVERB CLAUSE: *While **I was walking** to class, I ran into an old friend.*
    (b) MODIFYING PHRASE: *While **walking** to class, I ran into an old friend.*

(2) Or, if there is no **be** form of a verb, omit the subject and change the verb to **-ing.**

    (c) ADVERB CLAUSE: *Before **I left** for work, I ate breakfast.*
    (d) MODIFYING PHRASE: *Before **leaving** for work, I ate breakfast.*

An adverb clause can be changed to a modifying phrase ONLY WHEN THE SUBJECT OF THE ADVERB CLAUSE AND THE SUBJECT OF THE MAIN CLAUSE ARE THE SAME. A *modifying phrase* that is the reduction of an adverb clause *modifies the subject* of the main clause. No change is possible if the subjects of the adverb clause and the main clause are different.

    (e) CHANGE POSSIBLE: While **I** was sitting in class, **I** fell asleep.
                       While sitting in class, **I** fell asleep.

    (f) CHANGE POSSIBLE: While **Ann** was sitting in class, **she** fell asleep.
                       While sitting in class, **Ann** fell asleep.

    (g) NO CHANGE POSSIBLE: While **the teacher** was lecturing to the class, **I** fell asleep.*

    (h) NO CHANGE POSSIBLE: While **we** were walking home, **a frog** hopped across the road in front of us.

*"*While lecturing to the class, **I** fell asleep.*" means "*While **I** was lecturing to the class, **I** fell asleep.*"

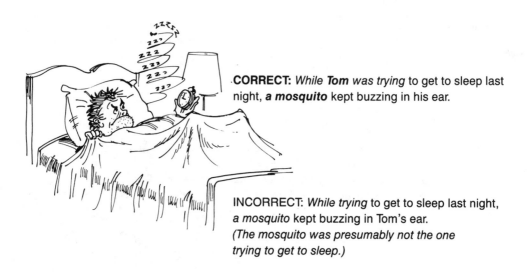

CORRECT: *While **Tom** was trying* to get to sleep last night, ***a mosquito** kept buzzing in his ear.*

INCORRECT: *While trying* to get to sleep last night, *a mosquito* kept buzzing in Tom's ear.
(The mosquito was presumably not the one trying to get to sleep.)

8-13 CHANGING TIME CLAUSES TO MODIFYING PHRASES

(a) CLAUSE: ***Since Mary came to this country***, she has made many friends. (b) PHRASE: ***Since coming to this country***, Mary has made many friends.	Adverb clauses beginning with ***after***, ***before***, ***while***, and ***since*** can be changed to modifying phrases.
(c) CLAUSE: ***After he (had) finished his homework***, he went to bed. (d) PHRASE: ***After finishing his homework***, he went to bed. (e) PHRASE: ***After having finished his homework***, he went to bed.	In (c): There is no difference in meaning between *After he finished* and *After he had finished*. (See Chart 1-17.) In (d) and (e): There is no difference in meaning between *After finishing* and *After having finished*.
(f) PHRASE: He went to bed ***after finishing his homework***.	A modifying phrase may follow the main clause, as in (f).

8-14 EXPRESSING THE IDEA OF "DURING THE SAME TIME" IN MODIFYING PHRASES

(a) ***While I was walking*** down the street, ***I*** ran into an old friend. (b) ***While walking*** down the street, ***I*** ran into an old friend. (c) ***Walking*** down the street, ***I*** ran into an old friend. (d) ***Hiking*** through the woods yesterday, ***we*** saw a bear. (e) ***Pointing*** to the sentence on the board, ***the teacher*** explained the meaning of modifying phrases.	Sometimes ***while*** is omitted but the ***-ing*** phrase at the beginning of the sentence gives the same meaning (i.e., "during the same time"). (a), (b), and (c) have the same meaning.

Walking across the icy road, *Adam* slipped and fell.

8–15 EXPRESSING CAUSE AND EFFECT RELATIONSHIPS IN MODIFYING PHRASES

(f) **Because she needed** some money to buy a book, **Sue** cashed a check. (g) **Needing** some money to buy a book, **Sue** cashed a check. (h) **Because he lacked** the necessary qualifications, **he** was not considered for the job. (i) **Lacking** the necessary qualifications, **he** was not considered for the job.	Often an **-ing** phrase at the beginning of a sentence gives the meaning of "because." (f) and (g) have the same meaning. **Because** is not used in a modifying phrase. It is omitted, but the resulting phrase expresses a cause and effect relationship.
(j) **Having seen** that movie before, **I don't want** to go again. (k) **Having seen** that movie before, **I didn't want** to go again.	**Having** + *past participle* gives the meaning not only of "because" but also of "before."
(l) **Because she was unable** to afford a car, **she** bought a bicycle. (m) **Being unable** to afford a car, **she** bought a bicycle. (n) **Unable** to afford a car, **she** bought a bicycle.	A form of **be** in the adverb clause is often changed to **being**. The use of **being** makes the cause and effect relationship clear.

8–16 USING *UPON* + *-ING* IN MODIFYING PHRASES

(a) **Upon reaching** the age of 21, I received my inheritance. (b) **When I reached** the age of 21, I received my inheritance.	Modifying phrases beginning with **upon** + **-ing** usually have the same meaning as adverb clauses introduced by **when**. (a) and (b) have the same meaning.
(c) **On reaching** the age of 21, I received my inheritance.	**Upon** can be shortened to **on**. (a), (b), and (c) all have the same meaning.

CHAPTER *9*

Showing Relationships Between Ideas—Part II

9–1 EXPRESSING UNEXPECTED RESULT: USING *EVEN THOUGH*

(a) ***Because*** the weather was cold, I *didn't go* swimming. (b) ***Even though*** the weather was cold, I *went* swimming. (c) ***Because*** I wasn't tired, I *didn't go* to bed. (d) ***Even though*** I wasn't tired, I *went* to bed.	***Because*** is used to express expected results. ***Even though*** is used to express unexpected results.
	Like ***because***, ***even though*** introduces an adverb clause.

9–2 SHOWING OPPOSITION (UNEXPECTED RESULT)

All of the following example sentences have the same meaning.		
ADVERB CLAUSES	*even though* *although* *though*	(a) ***Even though*** *it was cold*, I went swimming. (b) ***Although*** *it was cold*, I went swimming. (c) ***Though*** *it was cold*, I went swimming.
CONJUNCTIONS	*but . . . anyway* *but . . . still* *yet . . . still*	(d) It was cold, ***but*** I went swimming ***anyway***. (e) It was cold, ***but*** I ***still*** went swimming. (f) It was cold, ***yet*** I ***still*** went swimming.
TRANSITIONS	*nevertheless* *nonetheless* *however*	(g) It was cold. ***Nevertheless***, I went swimming. (h) It was cold. ***Nonetheless***, I went swimming. (i) It was cold. ***However***, I still went swimming.
PREPOSITIONS	*despite* *in spite of*	(j) I went swimming ***despite*** the cold weather. (k) I went swimming ***in spite of*** the cold weather.

9-3 SHOWING DIRECT OPPOSITION

ADVERB CLAUSES	*whereas* *while*	(a) Mary is rich, ***whereas*** *John is poor.* (b) Mary is rich, ***while*** *John is poor.* (c) John is poor, ***while*** *Mary is rich.* (d) ***Whereas*** *Mary is rich,* John is poor.	***Whereas*** and ***while*** are used to show direct opposition: "this" is exactly the opposite of "that." ***Whereas*** and ***while*** may be used with the idea of either clause with no difference in meaning. Note: A comma is usually used even if the adverb clause comes second.
CONJUNCTION	*but*	(e) Mary is rich, ***but*** John is poor. (f) John is poor, ***but*** Mary is rich.	In (e) through (j): As with ***whereas*** and ***while***, it does not make any difference which idea comes first and which idea comes second. The two ideas are directly opposite.
TRANSITIONS	*however* *on the other hand*	(g) Mary is rich; ***however***, John is poor. (h) John is poor; ***however***, Mary is rich. (i) Mary is rich. John, ***on the other hand***, is poor. (j) John is poor. Mary, ***on the other hand***, is rich.	

9-4 EXPRESSING CONDITIONS IN ADVERB CLAUSES: "*IF* CLAUSES"

(a) ***If it rains***, the streets get wet.	"***If*** clauses" (also called *adverb clauses of condition*) present possible conditions. The main clause expresses results. In (a): POSSIBLE CONDITION = *it rains* RESULT = *the streets get wet*
(b) *If it* ***rains*** *tomorrow,* I will take my umbrella.	A present tense, not a future tense, is used in an "***if*** clause" even though the verb in the "***if*** clause" may refer to a future event or situation, as in (b).★

WORDS THAT INTRODUCE ADVERB CLAUSES OF CONDITION ("*IF* CLAUSES"):		
if *whether or not* *even if*	*in case (that)* *in the event (that)* *unless*	*only if* *providing (that)* *provided (that)*

★See Chapter 10 for uses of other verb forms in sentences with "***if*** clauses."

9–5   ADVERB CLAUSES OF CONDITION: USING *WHETHER OR NOT* AND *EVEN IF*

WHETHER OR NOT (a) I'm going to go swimming tomorrow **whether or not it is cold**. (OR: **whether it is cold or not**.)	*Whether or not* expresses the idea that *neither this condition nor that condition matters*; the result will be the same. In (a): If it is cold, I'm going swimming. If it is not cold, I'm going swimming. I don't care about the temperature. It doesn't matter.
EVEN IF (b) I have decided to go swimming tomorrow. **Even if the weather is cold**, I'm going to go swimming.	Sentences with **even if** are close in meaning to those with **whether or not**. **Even if** gives the idea that a particular condition does not matter. The result will not change.
COMPARE: (c) **If** Ann studies hard, she *will pass* the exam. (d) **Even if** Mary studies hard, she *won't pass* the exam.	"**If** clauses" are followed by expected results, as in (c). CONDITION: *Ann studies* EXPECTED RESULT: *she passes the exam* "**Even if** clauses" are followed by unexpected results, as in (d). CONDITION: *Mary studies* UNEXPECTED RESULT: *she doesn't pass the exam*

9–6   ADVERB CLAUSES OF CONDITION: USING *IN CASE (THAT)* AND *IN THE EVENT (THAT)*

(a) I'll be at my uncle's house *in case you (should) need to reach me*. (b) **In the event that** *you (should) need to reach me*, I'll be at my uncle's house.	*In case that* and *in the event that* express the idea that something probably won't happen, but it might.* *in case/in the event that = if by any chance this should happen* Notes: *In the event that* is more formal than *in case*. The use of *should* in the adverb clause emphasizes the speaker's uncertainty that something will happen.

*In case that and *in the event that* introduce adverb clauses. *In case of* and *in the event of* have the same meaning, but they are prepositions followed by a noun object:
In case of trouble, call the police = In case (that) there is trouble, call the police.
In the event of rain, the picnic will be cancelled = In the event (that) it rains, the picnic will be cancelled.

9–7   ADVERB CLAUSES OF CONDITION: USING *UNLESS*

(a) I'll go swimming tomorrow **unless** *it's cold*. (b) I'll go swimming tomorrow **if** *it isn't cold*.	*unless = if . . . not* In (a): *unless it's cold = if it isn't cold* (a) and (b) have the same meaning.

9-8 ADVERB CLAUSES OF CONDITION: USING *ONLY IF* AND *PROVIDING/PROVIDED THAT*

(a) The picnic will be cancelled **only if it rains**. If it's windy, we'll go on the picnic. If it's cold, we'll go on the picnic. If it's damp and foggy, we'll go on the picnic. If it's unbearably hot, we'll go on the picnic.	**Only if** expresses the idea that there is only one condition that will cause a particular result.
(b) *Only if* it rains **will the picnic be cancelled**.	When **only if** begins a sentence, the subject and verb of the main clause are inverted, as in (b).
(c) **Providing/provided (that)** *no one has any further questions*, the meeting will be adjourned.	**Providing that** and **provided that** = *if* or *only if*.

9-9 EXPRESSING CONDITIONS: USING *OTHERWISE* AND *OR (ELSE)*

(a) I always eat breakfast. **Otherwise**, I get hungry during class. (b) You'd better hurry. **Otherwise**, you'll be late.	**Otherwise** expresses the idea "if the opposite is true, then there will be a certain result." In (a): *otherwise* = *if I don't eat breakfast* In (b): *otherwise* = *if you don't hurry*
(c) I always eat breakfast, **or (else)** I get hungry during class. (d) You'd better hurry, **or (else)** you'll be late.	**Or else** and **otherwise** have the same meaning. **Otherwise** is a transition. **Or (else)** is a conjunction.

- *If I don't wash my clothes*, I don't have clean clothes to wear. That's a truism.
- *If I don't wash my clothes tonight*, I won't have any clean clothes to wear tomorrow.
- *In the event that I decide not to wash my clothes tonight*, I won't have any clean clothes to wear tomorrow.
- *Unless I wash my clothes tonight*, I won't have any clean clothes to wear tomorrow.
- I will have to wear dirty clothes tomorrow *unless I wash my clothes tonight*.
- *Only if I wash my clothes tonight* will I have clean clothes to wear tomorrow.
- I'd better wash my clothes tonight. **Otherwise**, I'll have to wear dirty clothes tomorrow.

9–10 SUMMARY OF RELATIONSHIP WORDS: CAUSE AND EFFECT, OPPOSITION, CONDITION

	CAUSE & EFFECT	OPPOSITION	CONDITION
ADVERB CLAUSE WORDS	*because* *since* *now that* *as* *as/so long as* *inasmuch as* *so (that)*	*even though* *although* *though* *whearas* *while*	*if* *unless* *only if* *even if* *whether or not* *provided (that)* *providing (that)* *in case (that)* *in the event (that)*
TRANSITIONS	*therefore* *consequently*	*nevertheless* *nonetheless* *however* *on the other hand*	*otherwise*
CONJUNCTIONS	*so* *for*	*but* *yet*	*or (else)*
PREPOSITIONS	*because of* *due to*	*despite* *in spite of*	*in case of* *in the event of*

- Kate isn't paying attention to the stove **because** she is talking on the phone.
- Kate is talking on the phone. **Therefore,** she isn't paying attention to the stove.
- Kate isn't paying attention to the stove, **for** she is engrossed in her phone conversation.
- Kate is interested in her phone conversation, **so** she isn't paying attention to the stove.
- **Because of** her phone conversation, Kate isn't paying attention to the stove.
- **Even though** Kate smells smoke, she doesn't realize that her dinner is burning.
- Kate smells smoke. **However,** she doesn't pay attention to the stove.
- Kate smells smoke, **but** she keeps talking on the phone **anyway.**
- **Despite** the smell of smoke, Kate keeps talking on the phone.
- **If** Kate . . . . (see Chapter 10)

9–11 GIVING EXAMPLES

(a) There are many interesting places to visit in the city. **For example**, the botanical garden has numerous displays of plants from all over the world. (b) There are many interesting places to visit in the city. The art museum, **for instance**, has an excellent collection of modern paintings.	**For example** and **for instance** have the same meaning. They are often used as transitions.
(c) There are many interesting places to visit in the city, **e.g.**, the botanical garden and the art museum. (d) There are many interesting places to visit in the city, **for example**, the botanical garden or the art museum.	**e.g.** = for example (**e.g.** is an abbreviation of the Latin phrase *exempli gratia*.)★ (c) and (d) have the same meaning.
(e) I prefer to wear casual clothes, **such as** jeans and a sweatshirt. (f) Some countries, **such as** Brazil and Canada, are big. (g) Countries **such as** Brazil and Canada are big. (h) **Such** countries **as** Brazil and Canada are big.	**such as** = for example (f), (g), and (h) have essentially the same meaning even though the pattern varies.★★

*Punctuation note: Periods are used with **e.g.** in American English. Periods are generally not used with **eg** in British English.

**Punctuation note:
  (1) When the "**such as** phrase" can be omitted without substantially changing the meaning of the sentence, commas are used.
      Example: Some words, such as *know* and *see*, are verbs. (*Commas are used.*)
  (2) No commas are used when the "**such as** phrase" gives essential information about the noun to which it refers.
      Example: Words such as *know* and *see* are verbs. (*No commas are used.*)

9–12 CONTINUING THE SAME IDEA

(a) The city provides many cultural opportunities. It has an excellent art museum. ⎰ **Moreover,** ⎱ it has a fine ⎱ **Furthermore,** ⎰ ⎰ **In addition,** ⎱ symphony orchestra.	**Moreover**, **furthermore**, and **in addition** mean **also**. They are transitions.
(b) The city provides many cultural opportunities. ⎰ **In addition to** ⎱ an excellent art museum, it has a fine ⎱ **Besides** ⎰ symphony orchestra.	In (b): **In addition to** and **besides**★ are used as prepositions. They are followed by an object (*museum*), not a clause.

★COMPARE: **Besides** means *in addition to*.
         Beside means *next to*; e.g., *I sat beside my friend.*

CHAPTER *10*

Conditional Sentences

10–1 SUMMARY OF BASIC VERB FORM USAGE IN CONDITIONAL SENTENCES

MEANING OF THE "*IF* CLAUSE"	VERB FORM IN THE "*IF* CLAUSE"	VERB FORM IN THE "RESULT CLAUSE"	
True in the present/future	*simple present*	*simple present* *simple future*	(a) If I **have** enough time, I **write** to my parents every week. (b) If I **have** enough time tomorrow, I **will write** to my parents.
Untrue in the present/future	*simple past*	**would** + *simple form*	(c) If I **had** enough time now, I **would write** to my parents. (*In truth, I do not have enough time, so I will not write to them.*)
Untrue in the past	*past perfect*	**would have** + *past participle*	(d) If I **had had** enough time, I **would have written** to my parents yesterday. (*In truth, I did not have enough time, so I did not write to them.*)

- If Kate **pays** attention to the smell of smoke, she **will stop** talking on the phone.
- If Kate **knew** about the fire in the kitchen, she **would stop** talking on the phone immediately.
- If the phone **hadn't rung**, Kate **would not have left** the kitchen.

10-2 TRUE IN THE PRESENT OR FUTURE

(e) If I ***don't eat*** breakfast, I always ***get*** hungry during class.	In (e): The simple present is used in the result clause to express a habitual activity or situation.
(f) Water ***freezes (will freeze)*** if the temperature ***goes*** below 32°F/0°C.	In (f): Either the simple present or the simple future is used in the result clause to express an established, predictable fact.
(g) If I ***don't eat*** breakfast tomorrow morning, I ***will get*** hungry during class.	In (g) and (h): The simple future is used in the result clause when the sentence concerns a particular activity or situation in the future.
(h) If the weather ***is*** nice tomorrow, we ***will go*** on a picnic.	Note: The simple present, not the simple future, is used in the "***if*** clause."

10-3 UNTRUE (CONTRARY TO FACT) IN THE PRESENT/FUTURE

(i) If I ***taught*** this class, I ***wouldn't give*** tests.	In (i): In truth, I don't teach this class.
(j) If he ***were*** here right now, he ***would help*** us.	In (j): In truth, he is not here right now.
(k) If I ***were*** you, I ***would accept*** their invitation.	In (k): In truth, I am not you.
	Note: ***Were*** is used for both singular and plural subjects. ***Was*** (with *I*, *he*, *she*, *it*) is sometimes used in very informal speech but is not generally considered grammatically acceptable.

I ***would ride*** the roller coaster if those people ***didn't look*** scared to death. But those people look very scared, so I am not going to ride the roller coaster.

10-4   UNTRUE (CONTRARY TO FACT) IN THE PAST

(l) If you **had told** me about the problem, I **would have helped** you.	In (l): In truth, you did not tell me about it.
(m) If they **had studied**, they **would have passed** the exam.	In (m): In truth, they did not study. They failed the exam.
(n) If I **hadn't slipped** on the ice, **I wouldn't have broken** my arm.	In (n): In truth, I slipped on the ice. I broke my arm. Note: The auxiliary verbs are almost always contracted in speech. "If you'd told me, I would've helped you (OR: I'd've helped you)."

Mrs. Hook **wouldn't have driven** off if she **had known** that Tony's tie was caught in her car door.

10-5   USING PROGRESSIVE VERB FORMS

Notice the use of progressive verb forms in the following examples. Even in conditional sentences, progressive verb forms are used in progressive situations. (See Chart 1-2 for a discussion of progressive verbs.)

(a) TRUE:	It **is raining** right now, so I **will not go** for a walk.
(b) CONDITIONAL:	If it **were not raining** right now, I **would go** for a walk.
(c) TRUE:	I **am not living** in Chile. I **am not working** at a bank.
(d) CONDITIONAL:	If I **were living** in Chile, I **would be working** at a bank.
(e) TRUE:	It **was raining** yesterday afternoon, so I **did not go** for a walk.
(f) CONDITIONAL:	If it **had not been raining**, I **would have gone** for a walk.
(g) TRUE:	I **was not living** in Chile last year. I **was not working** at a bank.
(h) CONDITIONAL:	If I **had been living** in Chile last year, I **would have been working** at a bank.

If the beekeeper **were not wearing** protective clothing, she would get stung by the bees. It's a good thing that she is wearing special clothes.

10-6 USING "MIXED TIME" IN CONDITIONAL SENTENCES

Frequently the time in the "*if* clause" and the time in the "result clause" are different: One clause may be in the present and the other in the past. Notice that past and present times are mixed in the sentences in the following examples.

(a) TRUE:	I *did not eat* breakfast several hours ago, so I *am* hungry now.
(b) CONDITIONAL:	If I *had eaten* breakfast several hours ago, I *would not be* hungry now.
	(past) *(present)*
(c) TRUE:	He *is not* a good student. He *did not study* for the test yesterday.
(d) CONDITIONAL:	If he *were* a good student, he *would have studied* for the test.
	(present) *(past)*

There **wouldn't be** so many bugs in the room *this morning* if someone **had closed** the window *last night*.

10-7 USING *COULD, MIGHT,* AND *SHOULD*

(a) If I *were* a bird, I **could fly** home.	In (a): **could fly** = *would be able to fly*
(b) If I **could sing** as well as you, I *would join* the opera.	In (b): **could sing** = *were able to sing*
(c) If I'*d had* enough money, I **could have gone** to Florida for vacation.	In (c): **could have gone** = *would have been able to go*
(d) If I *don't get* a scholarship, I **might get** a job instead of going to graduate school next fall.	In (d): **I might get** = *maybe I will get*
(e) If you *were* a better student, you **might get** better grades.	In (e): **you might get** = *maybe you would get*
(f) If you *had told* me about your problem, I **might have been** able to help you.	In (f): **I might have been** = *maybe I would have been*
(g) If John **should call**, *tell* him I'll be back around five.	In (g): **If John should call** indicates a little more uncertainty or doubt than **If John calls**, but the meaning of the two is basically the same.
(h) If there **should be** another world war, the continued existence of the human race *would be* in jeopardy.	In (h): **If there should be** indicates more uncertainty or doubt than **If there were**.

10-8 OMITTING *IF*

(a) **Were I** you, I wouldn't do that.	With **were**, **had** (past perfect), and **should**, sometimes **if** is omitted and the subject and verb are inverted.
(b) **Had I known**, I would have told you.	In (a): **Were I you** = *If I were you*
(c) **Should anyone call**, please take a message.	In (b): **Had I known** = *If I had known*
	In (c): **Should anyone call** = *If anyone should call*

The cowboy shot at the snake, but he missed. **Had he killed** the snake, the snake couldn't have bitten his foot. **Were I** that cowboy, I would take shooting lessons. **Should he ever meet** another snake in the desert, he will need to know how to shoot straight.

It's lucky the cowboy was wearing boots. *Otherwise*, the snake's poisonous bite **would have killed** him. *Without boots*, the cowboy **would have died.**

10-9 IMPLIED CONDITIONS

(a) I **would have gone** with you, but I had to study. (*Implied condition*: . . . **if I hadn't had to study**)	Often the "*if* clause" is implied, not stated. Conditional verbs are still used in the "result clause."
(b) I never **would have succeeded** without your help. (*Implied condition*: . . . **if you hadn't helped me**)	
(c) She ran; *otherwise*, she **would have missed** her bus.	Conditional verbs are frequently used following **otherwise**. In (c), the implied "*if* clause" is: *If she had not run*. . . .

10–10 VERB FORMS FOLLOWING *WISH*

	VERB FORM IN "TRUE" SENTENCE	VERB FORM FOLLOWING *WISH*	
A wish about the future	(a) She *will not tell* me. (b) He *isn't going to be* here. (c) She *can't come* tomorrow.	I *wish* (that) she *would tell* me. I *wish* he *were going to be* here. I *wish* she *could come* tomorrow.	***Wish*** is used when the speaker wants reality to be different, to be exactly the opposite. Verb forms similar to those in conditional sentences are used. Notice the examples.
A wish about the present	(d) I *don't know* French. (e) It *is raining* right now. (f) I *can't speak* Japanese.	I *wish* I *knew* French. I *wish* it *weren't raining* right now. I *wish* I *could speak* Japanese.	
A wish about the past	(g) John *didn't come*. (h) Mary *couldn't come*.	I *wish* John *had come*.* I *wish* Mary *could have come*.	***Wish*** is followed by a noun clause. The use of ***that*** is optional. Usually it is omitted in speaking.

*Sometimes in very informal speaking: *I wish John **would have come**.*

Ben *wishes* it **weren't** so hot today. He *wishes* a cool breeze **were blowing**. He *wishes* the hot, humid weather **would change** soon. He *wishes* he **had bought** an air conditioner a long time ago.

10–11 USING *WOULD* TO MAKE WISHES ABOUT THE FUTURE

(a) It is raining. I *wish* it **would stop**. (*I want it to stop raining.*) (b) I'm expecting a call. I *wish* the phone **would ring**. (*I want the phone to ring.*)	***Would*** is usually used to indicate that the speaker *wants* something to happen in the future. The wish may or may not come true (be realized).
(c) It's going to be a good party. I *wish* you **would come**. (*I want you to come.*) (d) We're going to be late. I *wish* you **would hurry**. (*I want you to hurry.*)	In (c) and (d): ***I wish you would*** . . . is often used to make a request.

(a) It looks **like** *rain*.	Notice in (a): **like** is followed by a noun object.
(b) It looks **as if** *it is going to rain*.	Notice in (b) and (c): **as if** and **as though** are followed by a clause.
(c) It looks **as though** *it is going to rain*.	
(d) It looks **like** *it is going to rain*. (*informal*)	Notice in (d): **like** is followed by a clause. This use of **like** is common in informal English but is not generally considered appropriate in formal English. **As if** or **as though** is preferred. (a), (b), (c), and (d) all have the same meaning.

"TRUE" STATEMENT	VERB FORM AFTER *AS IF/AS THOUGH*	
(e) He **is not** a child.	She talked to him *as if* he **were** a child.	Usually the idea following **as if/as though** is "untrue." In this case, verb usage is similar to that in conditional sentences. Notice the examples.
(f) She **did not take** a shower with her clothes on.	When she came in from the rainstorm, she looked *as if* she **had taken** a shower with her clothes on.	
(g) He **has met** her.	He acted *as though* he **had never met** her.	
(h) She **will be** here.	She spoke *as if* she **wouldn't be** here.	

I know a farmer who talks to his animals **as if** they **were** people.

APPENDIX 1

Supplementary Grammar Units

UNIT A: Basic Grammar Terminology
UNIT B: Questions
UNIT C: Negatives
UNIT D: Articles

UNIT A: Basic Grammar Terminology

A-1 SUBJECTS, VERBS, AND OBJECTS

<table>
<tr>
<td>

    S   **V**
(a) ***Birds***   ***fly.***
  (NOUN) (VERB)

</td>
<td>

Almost all English sentences contain a subject (**S**) and a verb (**V**). The verb may or may not be followed by an object (**O**).

</td>
</tr>
<tr>
<td>

       S   **V**
(b) The ***baby*** ***cried.***
     (NOUN) (VERB)

</td>
<td>

VERBS: Verbs that are not followed by an object, as in (a) and (b), are called *intransitive verbs*. Common intransitive verbs: *agree, arrive, come, cry, exist, go, happen, live, occur, rain, rise, sleep, stay, wal*[.]

</td>
</tr>
<tr>
<td>

       S   **V**   **O**
(c) The ***student*** ***needs*** a ***pen.***
     (NOUN) (VERB) (NOUN)

      S   **V**   **O**
(d) My ***friend*** ***enjoyed*** the ***party.***
    (NOUN)   (VERB)   (NOUN)

</td>
<td>

Verbs that are followed by an object, as in (c) and (d), are called *transitive verbs*. Common transitive verbs: *build, cut, find, like, make, need, send, want.*

Some verbs can be either intransitive or transitive.
    intransitive: A student studies.
    transitive: A student studies books.

</td>
</tr>
<tr>
<td></td>
<td>

SUBJECTS AND OBJECTS: The subjects and objects of verbs are nouns (or pronouns). Examples of nouns: *person, place, thing, John, Asia, pen, information, appearance, amusement.*

</td>
</tr>
</table>

A-2 PREPOSITIONS AND PREPOSITIONAL PHRASES

COMMON PREPOSITIONS				
about	*before*	*despite*	*of*	*to*
above	*behind*	*down*	*off*	*toward(s)*
across	*below*	*during*	*on*	*under*
after	*beneath*	*for*	*out*	*until*
against	*beside*	*from*	*over*	*up*
along	*besides*	*in*	*since*	*upon*
among	*between*	*into*	*through*	*with*
around	*beyond*	*like*	*throughout*	*within*
at	*by*	*near*	*till*	*without*

(a) The student studies **in** **the library**. 　　S　　V　　PREP　O of PREP 　　　　　　　　　　　(NOUN)	An important element of English sentences is the prepositional phrase. It consists of a preposition (**PREP**) and its object (**O**). The object of a preposition is a noun or pronoun. In (a): **in the library** is a prepositional phrase.
(b) We enjoyed the party **at** **your house**. 　　S　V　　O　　PREP　O of PREP 　　　　　　　　　　　　　(NOUN)	
(c) We went **to the zoo** **in the afternoon**. 　　　　　(place)　　　　(time) (d) **In the afternoon**, we went to the zoo.	In (c): In most English sentences, "place" comes before "time." In (d): Sometimes a prepositional phrase comes at the beginning of a sentence.

A-3 ADJECTIVES

(a) Mary is an **intelligent** student. 　　　　　　　(ADJECTIVE)　(NOUN) (b) The **hungry** children ate fruit. 　　　(ADJECTIVE)(NOUN)	Adjectives describe nouns. In grammar, we say that adjectives modify nouns. The word *modify* means "change a little." Adjectives give a little different meaning to a noun: *intelligent student, lazy student, good student.* Examples of adjectives: *young, old, rich, poor, beautiful, brown, French, modern.*
(c) I saw some **beautiful** pictures. 　　*INCORRECT: beautifuls pictures*	An adjective is neither singular nor plural. A final **-s** is never added to an adjective.

The bees are **busy**.
The flowers are **beautiful**.

The **busy** bees are gathering nectar
from the **beautiful** flowers.

A-4 ADVERBS

(a) He walks **quickly**. 　　　　　　(ADVERB) (b) She opened the door **quietly**. 　　　　　　　　　　(ADVERB)	Adverbs modify verbs. Often they answer the question "*How?*" In (a): *How does he walk?* Answer: *Quickly.* Adverbs are often formed by adding **-ly** to an adjective. 　　*adjective:* **quick** 　　*adverb:* **quickly**
(c) I am **extremely** *happy*. 　　　(ADVERB) (ADJECTIVE)	Adverbs are also used to modify adjectives, i.e., to give information about adjectives, as in (c).
(d) Ann will come **tomorrow**. 　　　　　　　　(ADVERB)	Adverbs are also used to express time or frequency. Examples: *tomorrow, today, yesterday, soon, never, usually, always, yet.*
MIDSENTENCE ADVERBS (e) Ann **always** comes on time. (f) Ann is **always** on time. (g) Ann has **always** come on time. (h) *Does she* **always** *come on time?*	Some adverbs may occur in the middle of a sentence. Midsentence adverbs have usual positions; they (1) come in front of simple present and simple past verbs (except **be**), as in (e); (2) follow **be** (simple present and simple past), as in (f); (3) come between a helping verb and a main verb, as in (g). In a question, a midsentence adverb comes directly after the subject, as in (h).
COMMON MIDSENTENCE ADVERBS *ever, always, usually, often, frequently, generally, sometimes, occasionally, seldom, rarely, hardly ever, never, not ever, already, finally, just, probably*	

A-5 THE VERB *BE*

(a) John *is* **a student**. 　　(BE)　　(NOUN) (b) John *is* **intelligent**. 　　(BE)　　(ADJECTIVE) (c) John *was* **at the library**. 　　(BE)　(PREP. PHRASE)	A sentence with **be** as the main verb has three basic patterns: In (a): **be** + *a noun* In (b): **be** + *an adjective* In (c): **be** + *a prepositional phrase*
(d) Mary **is** *writing* a letter. (e) They **were** *listening* to some music. (f) That letter **was** *written* by Alice.	**Be** is also used as an auxiliary verb in progressive verb tenses and in the passive. In (d) **is** = *auxiliary;* **writing** = *main verb*

TENSE FORMS OF *BE*			
	SIMPLE PRESENT	SIMPLE PAST	PRESENT PERFECT
SINGULAR	*I* **am** *you* **are** *he, she, it* **is**	*I was* *you were* *he, she, it was*	*I* **have been** *you* **have been** *he, she, it* **has been**
PLURAL	*we, you, they* **are**	*we, you, they were*	*we, you, they* **have been**

A-6 LINKING VERBS

(a) The soup *smells* *good*.
       (LINKING VERB)   (ADJECTIVE)
(b) This food *tastes delicious*.
(c) The children *feel happy*.
(d) The weather *became cold*.
	Other verbs like *be* that may be followed immediately by an adjective are called *linking verbs*. An adjective following a linking verb describes the subject of a sentence.*
	
	Common verbs that may be followed by an adjective:
	    feel, look, smell, sound, taste
	    appear, seem
	    become (and *get, turn, grow* when they mean "become")

*COMPARE:
    (1) *The man looks angry.* → An adjective (*angry*) follows *look*. The adjective describes the subject (*the man*). *Look* has the meaning of "appear."
    (2) *The man looked at me angrily.* → An adverb (*angrily*) follows *look at*. The adverb describes the action of the verb. *Look at* has the meaning of "regard, watch."

A-7 PERSONAL PRONOUNS

	SINGULAR	PLURAL	

SUBJECT
PRONOUNS
	I
	you
	she, *he*, *it*
		we
		you
		they
			A pronoun is used in place of a noun. It refers to a noun. The noun it refers to is called the *antecedent*. *Examples:*
			    I read the *book*. *It* was good.
			(The pronoun "it" refers to the antecedent noun "book.")
			    Mary said, "*I* drink tea."
			(The pronoun "I" refers to the speaker, whose name is Mary.)

OBJECT PRONOUNS	*me* *you* *her*, *him*, *it*	*us* *you* *them*	
POSSESSIVE PRONOUNS	*mine* *your* *hers*, *his*	*ours* *yours* *theirs*	Possessive pronouns are not followed immediately by a noun; they stand alone. *Example:* That book is *mine*. Those are *yours* over there.*
POSSESSIVE ADJECTIVES	*my* name *your* name *her*, *his*, *its* name	*our* names *your* names *their* names	Possessive adjectives are followed immediately by a noun; they do not stand alone. *Example:* *My* book is here. *Your* books are over there.

*Possessive nouns require apostrophes; e.g., That book is *Mary's*. (See Chart 5-3.) Possessive pronouns do NOT take apostrophes.
    CORRECT: That book is *hers*, and those books are *theirs*.
    INCORRECT: That book is *her's* and those books are *theirs'*.

A-8 CONTRACTIONS

IN SPEAKING:	In everyday spoken English, certain forms of **be** and auxiliary verbs are usually contracted with pronouns, nouns, and question words.	
IN WRITING:	(1) In written English, contractions with pronouns are common in informal writing, but not generally acceptable in formal writing.	
	(2) Contractions with nouns and question words are, for the most part, rarely used in writing. A few of these contractions may be found in quoted dialogue in stories or in very informal writing, such as a chatty letter to a good friend, but most of them are rarely if ever written.	

In the following, quotation marks indicate that the contraction is frequently spoken but rarely if ever written.

	WITH PRONOUNS	WITH NOUNS	WITH QUESTION WORDS
am	*I'm* reading a book.	Ø	*"What'm"* I supposed to do?
is	*She's* studying. *It's* going to rain.	My *"book's"* on the table. *Mary's* at home.	*Where's* Sally? *Who's* that man?
are	*You're* working hard. *They're* waiting for us.	My *"books're"* on the table." The *"teachers're"* at a meeting.	*"What're"* you doing? *"Where're"* they going?
has	*She's* been here for a year. *It's* been cold lately.	My *"book's"* been stolen! *Sally's* never met him.	*Where's* Sally been living? *What's* been going on?"
have	*I've* finished my work. *They've* never met you.	The *"books've"* been sold. The *"students've"* finished the test."	*"Where've"* they been? *"How've"* you been?
had	*He'd* been waiting for us. *We'd* forgotten about it.	The *"books'd"* been sold. *"Mary'd"* never met him before.	*"Where'd"* you been before that? *"Who'd"* been there before you?
did	Ø	Ø	*"What'd"* you do last night? *"How'd"* you do on the test?
will	*I'll* come later. *She'll* help us.	The *"weather'll"* be nice tomorrow. *"John'll"* be coming soon.	*"Who'll"* be at the meeting? *"Where'll"* you be at ten?
would	*He'd* like to go there. *They'd* come if they could.	My *"friends'd"* come if they could. *"Mary'd"* like to go there, too.	*"Where'd"* you like to go?

"**Why're** you in my closet, Mr. Bear? **What're** you doing here?"

"I live here."

"**Where'd** you come from?"

"Your imagination."

"**How long're** you gonna stay?"

"As long as you want."

"Okay. **What'd** you like to do? Wanna play house?"

"Sure."

"Okay. You be the Papa Bear and I'll be the Momma Bear. But **who'll** be the Baby Bear?"

"I guess we'll just have to use our imaginations."

"Okay."

UNIT B: Questions

B-1   FORMS OF YES/NO AND INFORMATION QUESTIONS

A yes/no question	= a question that may be answered by *yes* or *no*. *Yes/no question:* Does he live in Chicago? *Answer:* Yes, he does. OR No, he doesn't.
An information question	= a question that asks for information by using a question word. *Information question:* Where does he live? *Answer:* In Chicago.

	QUESTION WORD	AUXILIARY VERB	SUBJECT	MAIN VERB		
(a) **She lives** there.	 Where	**Does** **does**	she she	live live?	there?	If the verb is in the simple present, use **does** (with *he, she, it*) or **do** (with *I, you, we, they*) in the question. If the verb is simple past, use **did**.
(b) **They live** there.	 Where	**Do** **do**	they they	live live?	there?	
(c) **He lived** there.	 Where	**Did** **did**	he he	live live?	there?	Notice: The main verb in the question is in its simple form; there is no final **-s** or **-ed**.
(d) **He is living** there.	 Where	**Is** **is**	he he	living living?	there?	If the verb has an auxiliary (a helping verb), the same auxiliary is used in the question. There is no change in the form of the main verb.
(e) **They have lived** there.	 Where	**Have** **have**	they they	lived lived?	there?	
(f) **Mary can live** there.	 Where	**Can** **can**	Mary Mary	live live?	there?	
(g) **He will be living** there.	 Where	**Will** **will**	he he	be living be living?	there?	If the verb has more than one auxiliary, only the first auxiliary precedes the subject.
(h) **John lives** there.	**Who**	Ø	Ø	lives	there?	If the question word is the subject, do not change the verb. Do not use **does**, **do**, or **did**.
(i) **Mary can come.**	**Who**	can	Ø	come?		
(j) **They are** there.	 Where	**Are** **are**	they they?		there?	**Be** in the simple present (*am, is, are*) and simple past (*was, were*) precedes the subject when **be** is the main verb.
(k) **Jim was** there.	 Where	**Was** **was**	Jim Jim?		there?	

B-2 QUESTION WORDS

	QUESTION	ANSWER	
WHEN	(a) **When** did they arrive? **When** will you come?	Yesterday. Next Monday.	**When** is used to ask questions about *time*.
WHERE	(b) **Where** is she? **Where** can I find a pen?	At home. In that drawer.	**Where** is used to ask questions about *place*.
WHY	(c) **Why** did he leave early? **Why** aren't you coming with us?	Because he's ill. I'm tired.	**Why** is used to ask questions about *reason*.
HOW	(d) **How** did you come to school? **How** does he drive?	By bus. Carefully.	**How** generally asks about *manner*.
	(e) **How much** money does it cost? **How many** people came?	Ten dollars. Fifteen.	**How** is used with **much** and **many**.
	(f) **How old** are you? **How cold** is it? **How soon** can you get here? **How fast** were you driving?	Twelve. Ten below zero. In ten minutes. 50 miles an hour.	**How** is also used with adjectives and adverbs.
	(g) **How long** has he been here? **How often** do you write home? **How far** is it to Miami from here?	Two years. Every week. 500 miles.	**How long** asks about *length of time*. **How often** asks about *frequency*. **How far** asks about *distance*.
WHO	(h) **Who** can answer that question? **Who** came to visit you?	I can. Jane and Eric.	**Who** is used as the subject of a question. It refers to people.
	(i) **Who is** coming to dinner tonight? **Who wants** to come with me?	Ann, Bob, and Al. We do.	**Who** is usually followed by a singular verb even if the speaker is asking about more than one person.
WHOM	(j) **Who(m)** did you see? **Who(m)** are you visiting? (k) **Who(m)** should I talk **to**? **To whom** should I talk? (*formal*)	I saw George. My relatives. The secretary.	**Whom** is used as the object of a verb or preposition. In spoken English, **whom** is rarely used; **who** is used instead. **Whom** is used only in formal questions. Note: **Whom**, not **who**, is used if preceded by a preposition.

	QUESTION	ANSWER	
WHOSE	(1) **Whose book** did you borrow? **Whose key** is this? (**Whose** is this?)	David's. It's mine.	**Whose** asks questions about *possession*.
WHAT	(m) **What** made you angry? **What** went wrong?	His rudeness. Everything.	**What** is used as the subject of a question. It refers to "things."
	(n) **What** do you need? **What** did Alice buy? (o) **What** did he talk **about**? **About what** did he talk? (*formal*)	I need a pencil. A book. His vacation.	**What** is also used as an object.
	(p) **What kind of** soup is that? **What kind of** shoes did he buy?	It's bean soup. Sandals.	**What kind of** asks about the particular variety or type of something.
	(q) **What did** you *do* last night? **What is** Mary *doing*?	I studied. Reading a book.	**What** + *a form of do* is used to ask questions about activities.
	(r) **What countries** did you visit? **What time** did she come? **What color** is his hair?	Italy and Spain. Seven o'clock. Dark brown.	**What** may accompany a noun.
	(s) **What is** Ed *like*? (t) **What is** the weather *like*?	He's kind and friendly. Hot and humid.	**What** + **be like** asks for a general description of qualities.
	(u) **What does** Ed *look like*? (v) **What does** her house *look like*?	He's tall and has dark hair. It's a two-story, red brick house.	**What** + **look like** asks for a physical description.
WHICH	(w) I have two pens. **Which pen** do you want? **Which one** do you want? **Which** do you want? (x) **Which book** should I buy?	The blue one. That one.	**Which** is used instead of **what** when a question concerns choosing from a definite, known quantity or group.
	(y) **Which countries** did he visit? **What countries** did he visit? (z) **Which class** are you in? **What class** are you in?	Peru and Chile. This class.	In some cases, there is little difference in meaning between **which** and **what** when they accompany a noun, as in (y) and (z).

B-3 NEGATIVE QUESTIONS

(a) ***Doesn't she live*** in the dormitory? (b) ***Does she not live*** in the dormitory? (*very formal*)	In a yes/no question in which the verb is negative, usually a contraction (e.g., *does + not = doesn't*) is used, as in (a). Example (b) is very formal and is usually not used in everyday speech. Negative questions are used to indicate the speaker's idea (i.e., what s/he believes is or is not true) or attitude (e.g., surprise, shock, annoyance, anger).

(c)   Bob returns to his dorm room after his nine o'clock class. Dick, his roommate, is there. Bob is surprised.
   Bob says: "*What are you doing here?* ***Aren't you supposed to be in class now?***"
(d)   Alice and Mary are at home. Mary is about to leave on a trip and Alice is going to take her to the airport.
   Alice says: "*It's already two o'clock. We'd better leave for the airport.* ***Doesn't your plane leave at three?***"
	In (c): Bob believes that Dick is supposed to be in class now.
	Expected answer: **Yes.**
	
	In (d): Alice believes that Mary's plane leaves at three. She is asking the negative question to make sure that her information is correct.
	Expected answer: **Yes.**

(e)   The teacher is talking to Jim about a test he failed. The teacher is surprised that Jim failed the test because he usually does very well.
   The teacher says: "*What happened?* ***Didn't you study?***"
(f)   Barb and Don are riding in a car. Don is driving. He comes to a corner where there is a stop sign, but he does not stop the car. Barb is shocked.
   Barb says: "*What's the matter with you?* ***Didn't you see that stop sign?***"
	In (e): The teacher believes that Jim did not study.
	Expected answer: **No.**
	
	In (f): Barb believes that Don did not see the stop sign.
	Expected answer: **No.**

"***Doesn't*** Ed realize he's putting ketchup in his coffee?"
"*No.*"
"***Isn't*** that a little strange?"
"*Yes.*"
"What's the matter with him?"
"I think he's in love."

B-4 TAG QUESTIONS

(a) Jack **can** come, **can't he?** (b) Fred **can't** come, **can he?**	A *tag question* is a question added at the end of a sentence. Speakers use tag questions chiefly to make sure their information is correct or to seek agreement.*

AFFIRMATIVE SENTENCE + NEGATIVE TAG	→ AFFIRMATIVE ANSWER EXPECTED
Mary **is** here, **isn't she?**	Yes, she is.
You **like** tea, **don't you?**	Yes, I do.
They **have left**, **haven't they?**	Yes, they have.

NEGATIVE SENTENCE + AFFIRMATIVE TAG	→ NEGATIVE ANSWER EXPECTED
Mary **isn't** here, *is* she?	No, she isn't.
You **don't** like tea, **do** you?	No, I don't.
They **haven't** left, **have** they?	No, they haven't.

(c) **This/That** is your book, isn't **it?** **These/Those** are yours, aren't **they?**	The tag pronoun for **this/that** = **it**. The tag pronoun for **these/those** = **they**.
(d) **There is** a meeting tonight, **isn't there?**	In sentences with **there** + **be**, **there** is used in the tag.
(e) **Everything** is okay, isn't **it?** (f) **Everyone** took the test, didn't **they?**	Personal pronouns are used to refer to indefinite pronouns. **They** is usually used in a tag to refer to **everyone, everybody, someone, somebody, no one, nobody.**
(g) **Nothing is** wrong, **is** it? (h) **Nobody called** on the phone, **did** they? (i) You**'ve never been** there, **have** you?	Sentences with negative words take affirmative tags.
(j) **I am** supposed to be here, **am I not?** (k) **I am** supposed to be here, **aren't I?**	In (j): **am I not?** is formal English. In (k): **aren't I?** is common in spoken English.

*A tag question may be spoken:
    (1) with a rising intonation if the speaker is truly seeking to ascertain that his/her information, idea, belief is correct (e.g., *Ann lives in an apartment, doesn't she?*); OR
    (2) with a falling intonation if the speaker is exressing an idea with which s/he is almost certain the listener will agree (e.g., *It's a nice day today, isn't it?*).

"*I warned* you not to touch the stove, **didn't I?**"
"Yes, Mom."
"*You touched* it anyway, **didn't you?**"
"Yes, Mom."
"*I've told* you never to touch a hot stove, **haven't I?**"
"Yes, Mom."
"*You won't* ever *touch* a hot stove again, **will you?**"
"No, Mom."
"Good. Now let me kiss your poor burned finger and make it all better, honey. Then we'll put some ointment on it."

UNIT C: Negatives

C-1 USING *NOT* AND OTHER NEGATIVE WORDS

(a) AFFIRMATIVE: The earth is round. (b) NEGATIVE: The earth is **not** flat.	**Not** expresses a *negative* idea.

AUX + *NOT* + MAIN VERB	**Not** immediately follows an auxiliary verb or *be*. (Note: If there is more than one auxiliary, **not** comes immediately after the first auxiliary: *I **will not** be going there.*)
(c) I **will** not go there. I **have** not gone there. I **am** not going there. I **was** not there. I **do** not go there. He **does** not go there. I **did** not go there.	**Do** or **does** is used with **not** to make a simple present verb (except **be**) negative. **Did** is used with **not** to make a simple past verb (except **be**) negative.

CONTRACTIONS OF AUXILIARY VERBS WITH *NOT*

are not = aren't*	do not = don't	must not = mustn't
cannot = can't	has not = hasn't	should not = shouldn't
could not = couldn't	have not = haven't	was not = wasn't
did not = didn't	had not = hadn't	were not = weren't
does not = doesn't	is not = isn't	will not = won't
		would not = wouldn't

(d) I **never** go there. I have **hardly ever** gone there.	In addition to **not**, the following are negative adverbs: *never, rarely, seldom* *hardly (ever), scarcely (ever), barely (ever)*
(e) There's **no** chalk in the drawer.	**No** also expresses a negative idea.

COMPARE: *NOT* vs. *NO*	**Not** is used to make a verb negative, as in (f).
(f) I **do not have** any money. (g) I have **no money**.	**No** is used as an adjective in front of a noun (e.g., **money**), as in (g). Note: (f) and (g) have the same meaning.

*Sometimes in spoken English you will hear "ain't." It means *am not, isn't,* or *aren't*. "Ain't" is not considered proper English, but many people use "ain't" regularly, and it is also frequently used for humor.

C-2 AVOIDING "DOUBLE NEGATIVES"

(a) *INCORRECT: I don't have no money.* (b) CORRECT: I **don't** have **any** money. CORRECT: I have **no** money.	(a) is an example of a "double negative," i.e., a confusing and grammatically incorrect sentence that contains two negatives in the same clause.* One clause should contain only one negative.

*NOTE: Negatives in two different clauses in the same sentence cause no problems; for example:
*A person who **doesn't** have love **can't** be truly happy.*
*I **don't** know why he **isn't** here.*

INCORRECT: Mike caught a boot, but he *didn't* catch *no* fish all day long.

   CORRECT: Mike caught a boot, but he *didn't* catch *any* fish all day long. OR:
   Mike caught a boot, but he *caught no* fish all day long.

C-3 BEGINNING A SENTENCE WITH A NEGATIVE WORD

(a) ***Never will I do*** that again. (b) ***Rarely have I eaten*** better food. (c) ***Hardly ever does he come*** to class on time.	When a negative word begins a sentence, the subject and verb are inverted (i.e., question word order is used).*

*Beginning a sentence with a negative word is relatively uncommon in everyday usage, but is used when the speaker/writer wishes to emphasize the negative element of the sentence.

UNIT D: Articles

D-1   BASIC ARTICLE USAGE

<table>
<tr><td colspan="3" align="center">I. USING A or Ø: GENERIC NOUNS</td></tr>
<tr>
<td>SINGULAR COUNT NOUN</td>
<td>(a) A banana is yellow.*</td>
<td rowspan="3">A speaker uses generic nouns to make generalizations. A generic noun represents a whole class of things; it is not a specific, real, concrete thing but rather a symbol of a whole group.

In (a) and (b): The speaker is talking about any banana, all bananas, bananas in general. In (c), the speaker is talking about any and all fruit, fruit in general.

Notice that no article (Ø) is used to make generalizations with plural count nouns and noncount nouns, as in (b) and (c).</td>
</tr>
<tr>
<td>PLURAL COUNT NOUN</td>
<td>(b) Ø Bananas are yellow.</td>
</tr>
<tr>
<td>NONCOUNT NOUN</td>
<td>(c) Ø Fruit is good for you.</td>
</tr>
<tr><td colspan="3" align="center">II. USING A or SOME: INDEFINITE NOUNS</td></tr>
<tr>
<td>SINGULAR COUNT NOUN</td>
<td>(d) I ate a banana.</td>
<td rowspan="3">Indefinite nouns are actual things (not symbols), but they are not specifically identified.

In (d): The speaker is not referring to "this banana" or "that banana" or "the banana you gave me." The speaker is simply saying that s/he ate one banana. The listener does not know nor need to know which specific banana was eaten; it was simply one banana out of that whole group of things in this world called bananas.

In (e) and (f): Some is often used with indefinite plural count nouns and indefinite noncount nouns. In addition to some, a speaker might use two, a few, several, a lot of, etc., with plural count nouns, or a little, a lot of, etc., with noncount nouns. (See Chart 5-8.)</td>
</tr>
<tr>
<td>PLURAL COUNT NOUN</td>
<td>(e) I ate some bananas.</td>
</tr>
<tr>
<td>NONCOUNT NOUN</td>
<td>(f) I ate some fruit.</td>
</tr>
<tr><td colspan="3" align="center">III. USING THE: DEFINITE NOUNS</td></tr>
<tr>
<td>SINGULAR COUNT NOUN</td>
<td>(g) Thank you for the banana.</td>
<td rowspan="3">A noun is definite when both the speaker and the listener are thinking about the same specific thing.

In (g): The speaker uses the because the listener knows which specific banana the speaker is talking about, i.e., that particular banana which the listener gave to the speaker.

Notice that the is used with both singular and plural count nouns and with noncount nouns.</td>
</tr>
<tr>
<td>PLURAL COUNT NOUN</td>
<td>(h) Thank you for the bananas.</td>
</tr>
<tr>
<td>NONCOUNT NOUN</td>
<td>(i) Thank you for the fruit.</td>
</tr>
</table>

*Usually **a/an** is used with a singular generic count noun. Examples: **A window** is made of glass. **A doctor** heals sick people. Parents must give **a child** love. **A box** has six sides. **An apple** can be red, green, or yellow.

The is sometimes used with a singular generic count noun (not a plural generic count noun, not a generic noncount noun). "Generic **the**" is commonly used with, in particular:

    (1) species of animals: **The whale** is the largest mammal on earth. **The elephant** is the largest land mammal.

    (2) inventions: Who invented the telephone? the wheel? the refrigerator? the airplane?
           The computer will play an increasingly large role in all of our lives.

    (3) musical instruments: I'd like to learn to play **the piano**. Do you play **the guitar**?

D-2 GENERAL GUIDELINES FOR ARTICLE USAGE

(a) **The sun** is bright today. Please hand this book to **the teacher**. Please open **the door**. Jack is in **the kitchen**.	GUIDELINE: Use **the** when you know or assume that your listener is familiar with and thinking about the same specific thing or person you are talking about.
(b) Yesterday I saw *some dogs*. **The dogs** were chasing *a cat*. **The cat** was chasing *a mouse*. **The mouse** ran into *a hole*. **The hole** was very small.	GUIDELINE: Use **the** for the second mention of an indefinite noun⋆; in (b): first mention = *some dogs, a cat, a mouse, a hole* second mention = *the dogs, the cat, the mouse, the hole*
(c) *INCORRECT:* *The apples are my favorite fruit.* *CORRECT:* **Apples** are my favorite fruit. (d) *INCORRECT:* *The gold is a metal.* *CORRECT:* **Gold** is a metal.	GUIDELINE: Do not use **the** with a plural count noun (e.g., *apples*) or a noncount noun (e.g., *gold*) when you are making a generalization.
(e) *INCORRECT:* *I drove car.* *CORRECT:* I drove **a car**. I drove **the car**. I drove **that car**. I drove **his car**.	GUIDELINE: Do not use a singular count noun (e.g., *car*) without: (1) an article (**a/an** or **the**); OR (2) **this/that**; OR (3) a possessive pronoun.

APPENDIX 2
Preposition Combinations

Appendix 2 contains two lists of preposition combinations. The first list consists of preposition combinations with adjectives and verbs. The second list contains phrasal verbs.

    These lists contain only those preposition combinations used in the exercises in the text and in the accompanying workbooks.

LIST 1: PREPOSITION COMBINATIONS WITH ADJECTIVES AND VERBS

A   *be* absent from
        accuse of
     be accustomed to
     be aquainted with
     be addicted to
     be afraid of
         agree with
     be angry at, with
     be annoyed with
         apologize for
         apply to, for
         approve of
         argue with, about
         arrive in, at
     be associated with
     be aware of

B   believe in
      blame for
   e blessed with
   ? bored with

C   *be* capable of
         care about, for
     be cluttered with
     be committed to
         compare to, with
         complain about
     be composed of
     be concerned about
     be connected to
         consist of
     be content with
         contribute to
     be convinced of
     be coordinated with
         count (up)on
         cover with
     be crowded with

D   decide (up)on
     be dedicated to
         depend (up)on

be devoted to
be dissapointed in, with
be discriminated against
distinguish from
be divorced from
be done with
dream of, about
be dressed in

E *be* engaged to
be envious of
be equipped with
escape from
excel in
be excited about
excuse for
be exposed to

F *be* faithful to
be familiar with
feel like
fight for
be filled with
be finished with
be fond of
forget about
forgive for
be friendly to, with
be furnished with

G *be* grateful to, for
be guilty of

H hide from
hope for

I *be* innocent of
insist (up)on
be interested in
be involved in

J *be* jealous of

K *be* known for

L *be* limited to
look forward to

M *be* made of, from
be married to

O object to
be opposed to

P participate in
be patient with
be polite to
pray for
be prepared for
prevent from
prohibit from
protect from
be provided with
be proud of
provide with

R recover from
be related to
be relevant to
rely (up)on
be remembered for
rescue from
respond to
be responsible for

S *be* satisfied with
be scared of
stare at
stop from
subscribe to
substitute for
succeed in

T take advantage of
take care of
be terrified of
thank for
be tired of, from

U *be* upset with
be used to

V vote for

W *be* worried about

LIST 2: PHRASAL VERBS (TWO-WORD AND THREE-WORD VERBS)

The term *phrasal verb* refers to a verb and preposition which together have a special meaning. For example, **put + off** means "postpone." Sometimes a phrasal verb consists of three parts. For example, **put + up + with** means "tolerate." Phrasal verbs are also called *two-word verbs* or *three-word verbs*.

SEPARABLE PHRASAL VERBS (a) I **handed** my paper **in** yesterday. (b) I **handed in** my paper yesterday.	A phrasal verb may be either *separable* or *nonseparable*. With a separable phrasal verb, a noun may come either between the verb and the preposition or after the preposition, as in (a) and (b).
(c) I **handed** it **in** yesterday. (INCORRECT: I handed in it yesterday.)	A pronoun comes between the verb and the preposition if the phrasal verb is separable, as in (c).
NONSEPARABLE PHRASAL VERBS (d) I **ran into** an old friend yesterday. (e) I **ran into** her yesterday. (INCORRECT: I ran an old friend into.) (INCORRECT: I ran her into yesterday.)	With a nonseparable phrasal verb, a noun or pronoun must follow the preposition, as in (d) and (e).

Phrasal verbs are especially common in informal English. Following is a list of common phrasal verbs and their usual meanings. This list contains only those phrasal verbs used in the exercises in the text. The phrasal verbs marked with an asterisk (*) are nonseparable.

A ask out . . . . *ask someone to go on a date*

B bring about, bring on . . . . *cause*
  bring up . . . . *(1) rear children; (2) mention or introduce a topic*

C call back . . . . *return a telephone call*
  call in . . . . *ask to come to an official place for a specific purpose*
  call off . . . . *cancel*
  *call on . . . . *(1) ask to speak in class; (2) visit*
  call up . . . . *call on the telephone*
  *catch up (with) . . . . *reach the same position or level*
  *check in, check into . . . . . *register at a hotel*
  *check into . . . . *investigate*
  check out . . . . *(1) take a book from the library; (2) investigate*
  *check out (of) . . . . *leave a hotel*
  cheer up . . . . *make (someone) feel happier*
  clean up . . . . *make clean and orderly*
  *come across . . . . *meet by chance*
  cross out . . . . *draw a line through*
  ͜ut . . . . *stop an annoying activity*

D do over . . . . *do again*
     *drop by, drop in (on) . . . . *visit informally*
     drop off . . . . *leave something/someone at a place*
     *drop out (of) . . . . *stop going to school, to a class, to a club, etc.*

F figure out . . . . *find the answer by reasoning*
     fill out . . . . *write the completions of a questionnaire or official form*
     find out . . . . *discover information*

G *get along (with) . . . . *exist satisfactorily*
     get back . . . . *(1) return from a place; (2) receive again*
     *get in, get into . . . . *(1) enter a car; (2) arrive*
     *get off . . . . *leave an airplane, a bus, a train, a subway, a bicycle*
     *get on . . . . *enter an airplane, a bus, a train, a subway, a bicycle*
     *get out of . . . . *(1) leave a car; (2) avoid work or an unpleasant activity*
     *get over . . . . *recover from an illness*
     *get through . . . . *finish*
     *get up . . . . *arise from bed, a chair*
     give back . . . . *return an item to someone*
     give up . . . . *stop trying*
     *go over . . . . *review or check carefully*
     *grow up (in) . . . . *become an adult*

H hand in . . . . *submit an assignment*
     hang up . . . . *(1) conclude a telephone conversation; (2) put clothes on a hanger or a hook*
     have on . . . . *wear*

K keep out (of) . . . . *not enter*
     *keep up (with) . . . . *stay at the same position or level*
     kick out (of) . . . . *force (someone) to leave*

L *look after . . . . *take care of*
     *look into . . . . *investigate*
     *look out (for) . . . . *be careful*
     look over . . . . *review or check carefully*
     look up . . . . *look for information in a reference book*

M make up . . . . *(1) invent; (2) do past work*

N name after, name for . . . . *give a baby the name of someone else*

P *pass away . . . . *die*
     pass out . . . . *(1) distribute; (2) lose consciousness*
     pick out . . . . *select*
     pick up . . . . *(1) go to get someone (e.g., in a car); (2) take in one's hand*
     point out . . . . *call attention to*

put away	. . . .	*remove to a proper place*
put back	. . . .	*return to original place*
put off	. . . .	*postpone*
put on	. . . .	*put clothes on one's body*
put out	. . . .	*extinguish a cigarette or cigar*
*put up with	. . . .	*tolerate*

R   *run into, *run across . . . .   *meet by chance*
    *run out (of) . . . .   *finish a supply of something*

S   *show up . . . .   *appear, come*
    shut off . . . .   *stop a machine, light, faucet*

T   *take after . . . .   *resemble*
    take off . . . .   *(1) remove clothing; (2) leave on a trip*
    take out . . . .   *(1) take someone on a date; (2) remove*
    take over . . . .   *take control*
    take up . . . .   *begin a new activity or topic*
    tear down . . . .   *demolish; reduce to nothing*
    tear up . . . .   *tear into many little pieces*
    think over . . . .   *consider carefully*
    throw away, throw out . . .   *discard; get rid of*
    throw up . . . .   *vomit; regurgitate food*
    try on . . . .   *put on clothing to see if it fits*
    turn down . . . .   *decrease volume or intensity*
    turn in . . . .   *(1) submit an assignment; (2) go to bed*
    turn off . . . .   *stop a machine, light, faucet*
    turn on . . . .   *begin a machine, light, faucet*
    turn out . . . .   *extinguish a light*
    turn up . . . .   *increase volume or intensity*

APPENDIX 3
Guide for Correcting Writing Errors

To the student: Each number represents an area of usage. Your teacher will use these numbers when marking your writing to indicate that you have made an error. Refer to this list to find out what kind of error you have made and then make the necessary correction.

1	SINGULAR-PLURAL	He have been here for six month.① ① *He has been here for six months.*
2	WORD FORM	I saw a beauty picture.② *I saw a beautiful picture.*
3	WORD CHOICE	She got on the taxi.③ *She got into the taxi.*
4	VERB TENSE	He is here since June.④ *He has been here since June.*
5+	ADD A WORD	I want ∧ go to the zoo.⑤+ *I want to go to the zoo.*
5−	OMIT A WORD	She entered to the university.⑤− *She entered the university.*
6	WORD ORDER	I saw five times that movie.⑥ *I saw that movie five times.*

7	INCOMPLETE SENTENCE	⑦ I went to bed. Because I was tired. *I went to bed because I was tired.*
8	SPELLING	⑧ An accident occured. *An accident occurred.*
9	PUNCTUATION	⑨ What did he say. *What did he say?*
10	CAPITALIZATION	⑩ I am studying english. *I am studying English.*
11	ARTICLE	⑪ I had a accident. *I had an accident.*
12?	MEANING NOT CLEAR	⑫? He borrowed some smoke. *(? ? ?)*
13	RUN-ON SENTENCE*	⑬ My roommate was sleeping, we didn't want to wake her up. *My roommate was sleeping. We didn't want to wake her up.*

on sentence occurs when two sentences are incorrectly connected: the end of one
e and the beginning of the next sentence are not properly marked by a period and a
letter or by a semicolon. (See Charts 8-3 and 8-9.)

Index

*The abbreviations "*fn.*" means "footnote." A footnote is found at the bottom of a chart or a page. Footnotes contain additional information.